# fortresses

# Hundred Years War Castles

## Stéphane William GONDOIN

*Translated from the French by Lawrence BROWN*

*General Editor Yann KERVRAN*

*Histoire & Collections*

**Tower Maubergeon. Castle of Poitiers.**

*All photographs by the author, except where mentioned*
*Drawings by Denis Gandilhon and Aurore Mathieu*

Supervision by Denis GANDILHON and Jean-Marie MONGIN—Design and lay-out by Jean-Marie MONGIN
© Histoire & Collections 2007

ISBN: 978-2-915239-80-5

Publisher's number: 915239

© Histoire & Collections 2007

A book published by
*HISTOIRE & COLLECTIONS*
SA au capital de 182 938, 82 €
5, avenue de la République F-75541 Paris Cédex 11
France
TéL. 01 40 21 18 20 - Fax 01 47 00 51 11
www.histoireetcollections.fr

This book has been designed, typed,
laid-out and processed by
*Histoire & Collections*
and *Studio A&C*
fully on integrated
computer equipment.

Printed by Zure,
Spain, European Union
*February 2007*

# Contents

# The fortresses collection

 HE FORTRESS CASTLE is the architectural element that springs to mind when we think about the Middle Ages. There was not a single territory in France that did expand without being in the shadow of a wall flanked with towers.

Crenels, machicolations and draw-bridges have become the principal visual elements that have attached themselves to the historical reality. Despite this heavy presence in our minds and in what we see, the history of their creation, development and deployment of architectural solutions is constantly being re-written.

A new viewpoint, since the pioneering work of the XIXth century, enables a regular updating of new hypothesis and to look at these familiar constructions in a different light.

Stéphane William Gondoin has tirelessly toured these fortresses for many years and shares here a personal synthesis that is the result of much research and many visits. This familiar viewpoint on the constructions that sheltered, or repulsed our medieval ancestors, is owed to the many long hours spent visiting curtain walls and keeps, and also to the carefully shot photographs that illustrate this book.

In this first volume, we invite you to discover these stone giants, to learn about their turbulent history, when the French and the English fought each other for the power of the royal crown during the Hundred Years War. Thanks to previous experimentations, the castles of the period were able to combine the needs imposed on them by the situation of almost permanent war, and the refined tastes of the powerful.

I hope that you will enjoy this book,

*Yann Kervran*
General Editor

**The castle of Andlau (Bas-Rhin).**
*(Photo Wild)*

# « Les lys ne filent pas »

"Fleurs de Lys do not spin"

Dont, puissedi, grant guerre et grant désolation
avint au royaume de France en pluisieurs pars,
si com vos porés oïr en ceste hystore.[1]

Froissart

HARLES IV, the last son of Phillip IV the Fair (1285-1314), died without leaving an heir, on February 1st, 1328. Thus began, in France, a period of uncertain succession: since the advent of Hughes Capet in 987, the crown had never slipped out of the hands of one of the sons or brothers of a dead king.

It now fell to the highest barons and prelates in the kingdom to draw up the modes of succession and find a new king. It was out of the question, in their minds, to offer the throne to a woman.

Five important personalities debating the succession of Charles IV the Fair (1328). Interior edging, illuminated initial. Grandes Chroniques de France, circa 1380.
*(Bibl. mun. de Lyon, Ms P.A. 30 f° 349.*
*Photograph Bibliothèque municipale de Lyon, Didier Nicole)*

## A land without a king.

The sceptre could, due to an uncontrolled marriage, fall into the wrong hands. Eleanor of Aquitaine's precedent of bringing her enormous duchy to Henri Plantagenet, under the very nose of Louis VII the Young (1152), had left a still painful memory. Moreover, the King held the position of supreme commander in times of war and this did not suit, according to the attitude of the time, a member of the fairer sex. The prospect of turning to the young king of England, Edward III, was not met with any more enthusiasm. He was, however, the only grandson of Phillip the Fair, by his mother, Isabelle de France. As Froissart said, *"the kingdom of France is made of such high nobility that it cannot go to a woman, nor, by consequence, to the son, meaning a successor, of a woman"*. The archbishop Jean de Marigny, tersely summed up with a *"Fleur de Lys* (french royal lilies) *do not spin"*. More to the point, the nobility did not want an English monarch. All this meant that a king had to be found amongst the other close male relatives of Charles. One name stood out immediately, that of Phillip de Valois, the first cousin of Charles. He was elected by the twelve peers of France after lengthy negotiations. He was anointed at Reims, May 29, 1328.

This decision was initially well received across the channel. Edward even accepted to pay homage for the Guyenne, the last strip of the Plantagenet continental empire still in the hands of its prestigious lineage. However, the situation in which a king finds himself vassal to another cannot stay serene for long. Very quickly, the relations between the two monarchies became poisoned. Valois openly supported the Scottish in their never-ending struggle against the government of London.

He also intervened regularly in Flemish affairs. Flanders was the main outlet for English wool. Edward saw, in the aggressive attitude of his cousin, a major threat to his economic interests, he made the most of the opportunity to remind him of his right to the French throne. From 1336, he started to rally support of those hostile to Phillip. In 1337, Valois decided to confiscate the Duchy of Guyenne for disloyalty. The break had now been confirmed and war was inevitable.

This growing conflict between two large European nations can doubtlessly be seen as the last convulsion of a dying feudal world. Jacques Le Goff said. *" In France, as in England, the nobility, looking for a new balance in the face of a cash economy, the changes in the feudal income, the growth of the towns and the power of the monarchy, looked towards war as a solution to their problems."*

---

1. *"Therefore, from this day, a great war and great evils fell upon the whole kingdom of France, as you will hear in this story."*

# The legal imbroglio

**T**HE FUNDAMENTAL question revolves around the right of women to pass on the crown.

If this possibility is accepted, Jeanne de Navarre, Louis X the Hutin's wife, is the first in the line of succession. There were, however, heavy suspicions of her illegitimate origins and she was still without a son in 1328 (Charles the Bad, future king of Navarre was born four years later). Following next were all of Phillip V's daughters, then the little Blanche posthumously born to Charles IV. Only then came Edward III, son of Isabelle de France.

Phillip de Valois was seen as the only alternative in the eyes of the French peers. His candidacy did not immediately win support and long negotiations and intense dealing lead up to his election.

The noblemen looked favourably at the idea of placing one of their own on the throne, with him thus becoming indebted to them.

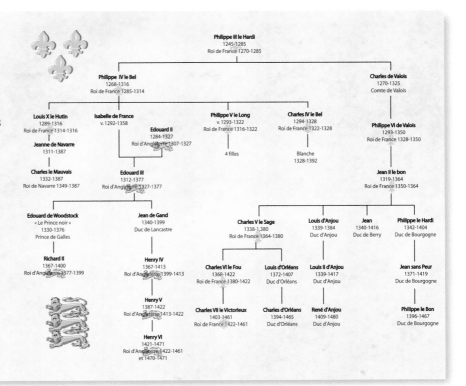

## The first French setbacks

The kingdom of France at the time had a population of nearly 15 million, whereas its adversary had only 5 million, France was, however, beset by internal quarrels. There was not yet permanent institutionalised taxation and the King always had to fight to obtain more money. There was also no professional army. Edward, on the other hand, managed to obtain large grants from Lombardy bankers and had professional troops at his disposal, who had gained much experience in the fighting against the Welsh and the Scots during the last decades.

The war began by indirect clashes in Flanders. England feared a French invasion, a fear that was reinforced by a bloody raid on Southampton in 1339. Maritime superiority would be the key to final victory, both sides were convinced of this. On June 24, 1340, at Sluys, the forward port of Bruges, the French and English fleets met. The outcome was of total disaster for Valois with 90% of his units sent to the bottom of the sea. The English now controlled the Channel; the fighting would take place on French soil.

Edward III landed in Saint-Vaast-la-Hougue in the north of the Cotentin peninsula on July 12, 1346 and the surrounding land was laid waste. The English rapidly moved on Caen which was taken and devastated. Their trail continued via Rouen, crossing the Seine at Poissy and moving north towards the Somme. This time, King Phillip was

**The Merle Towers.**

7

*Opposite.*
**The siege of Tournai by Edward III in 1340. The Hundred Years War begins with indirect confrontations outside the fighting nations. The inhabitants take shelter behind their walls. Jean Froissart's Chronicles, 2nd quarter of the XVth century.**
*(Paris, Bibl. nat. de France Ms. Fr. 2675 f° 74)*

spoiling for a fight. He gathered his troops, raised his standard, and began the pursuit of the invader. He caught up with the English at Crècy-en-Ponthieu. The English would now discover the price to pay for attacking the kingdom of the "lys"! However, badly prepared and totally lacking in discipline, the French knights, even though a superior force, were cut to pieces by the English archers (August 26, 1346).

Valois would never recover from this crushing defeat.

### "Great evils fell upon the whole kingdom"

Edward's next move was north to Calais which he took after a siege of several months (1347). The town now gave him a solid bridgehead from which he could lead expeditions into enemy territory. The war seemed destined to go on forever; hostilities, however, only restarted nine years later. Another enemy lurked in the shadows and struck both sides.

People began dying of a strange illness around Marseille. It had almost been forgotten. The Black Death was back. Spreading everywhere, it reached the northern parts of the kingdom and England, forcing both sides into a period of inactivity. Between a quarter and a third of the population fell victim to the Black Death which, from

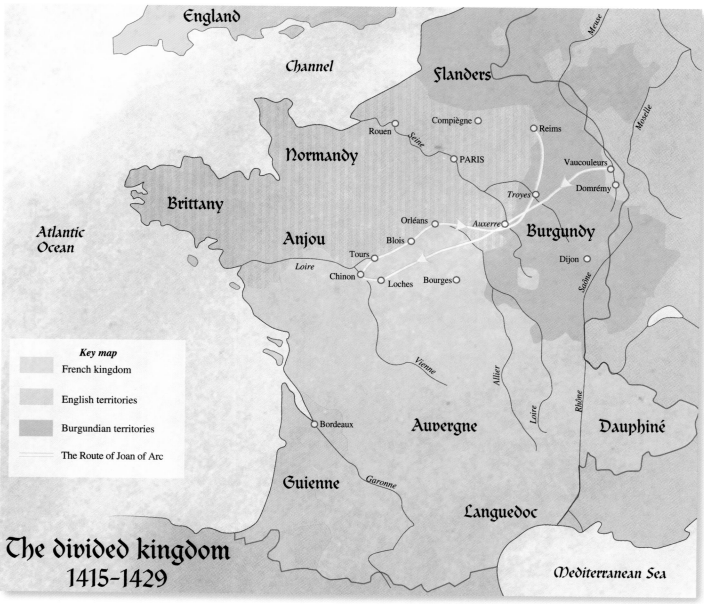

**The divided kingdom 1415-1429**

*Key map*

French kingdom

English territories

Burgundian territories

The Route of Joan of Arc

now on, reappeared regularly to decimate the land between two periods of famine… a case of one disaster after an other.

Hostilities resumed in 1355. Jean II had replaced his father, Phillip VI, who had died August 22, 1350. Under the command of Edward's eldest son, known to posterity as the Black Prince, the English stirred again in the Languedoc. In 1356, they launched a raid in the Poitou. Jean moved to meet the English with his army and caught up with them at Maupertuis, near Poitiers. Lessons, however, had been learnt from the past… At Crécy, the cavalry attacks had proved ineffective. They would, therefore, charge… on foot! The punishment was immediate and identical. The flower of French knighthood, freshly reformed, was once more cut down. Worse still, the King himself fell into enemy hands. After a few renewable annual truces, Valois had to agree to the humiliating treaty of Brétigny (1360). Officially renouncing the French crown, Edward received, in return, all of the Aquitaine as full sovereign, as well as Ponthieu, Guines and Calais. France also had to pay the enormous sum of 3,000,000 gold ecus for the royal ransom. Jean was freed against the deposit of 400,000 ecus and the release of several important hostages. The escape of one of these, his son Louis of Anjou, meant that the King, with an undeniable sense of honour but lacking in political talent, had to return to England where he passed away on April 8, 1364.

## *"Bonnes mœurs du sage roi Charles"*
*(the chivalresque and wise King Charles)*

Charles, eldest of Jean the Good, soon showed himself to be of a different moral fibre. He was certainly not the model of a chivalresque king. He suffered from many physical defects and was not attracted by the sword. His undeniable clear sightedness, however, whilst his father was held captive, allowed him to deal with the Paris revolt led by the vindictive Étienne Marcel and also foil the schemes of his cousin Charles the Bad, king of Navarre. It was, therefore, an accomplished man that now donned the crown. Charles also knew how to surround himself with the right people: Du Guesclin being the most famous of his many supporters.

The first thing to do was rid the country of the roaming troops that infested it. That was no problem! They were sent to fight in the Castille under the command of Bertrand du Guesclin and Ernoul d'Audrehem. Valois and Plantagenet then began to clash indirectly in Ponthieu and in Armagnac. From 1369, total war resumed. Charles denounced the terms of the treaty of Brétigny and Edward demanded the rest of the ransom that had never been paid. The English began

Jean II le Bon (John the Good), King Edward III's prisoner in London (1364). The defeat at Poitiers (1356) had farther-reaching consequences than those of Crécy (1346), due to the capture of the French king. Edward wears a cloak bearing the three golden English leopards on a red gule background. Jean wears a pelisse bearing the emblem of France (gold fleurs de lys on an azure background). Jean Froissart's Chronicles, early XVth century.
*(Bibl. mun. de Besançon, Ms 864 f° 235. Photograph CNRS-IRHT)*

once more the long chevauchées, laying waste and pillaging the country. The French systematically avoided all-out confrontation and took refuge in strongholds, preferring harassing tactics. Their enemy exhausted themselves in vain, then retreated. The death of the Black Prince (1376), followed shortly after by Edward III (1377) and Richard II's minority, made things easier for the Valois. In 1380 he ruled over the bigger part of the Aquitaine. His biographer, Christine de Pisan, could not stop singing his praises concerning his successes: *"King Charles was a chivalresque Prince, a wise man, defender and guardian of his people."*

# Messire Jean Froissart

**JEAN FROISSART was born into a Valenciennes family around 1337.**

Close to Philippa de Hainaut, Edward III's wife, he wrote, probably from 1370, his immense *Chroniques de France, d'Angleterre et des pais voisins*. The lively and colourful account covers almost a century of conflictual relations between the lys and the leopard (1327-1400).

It is our best source of information on the first half of the Hundred Years War. Froissart is also known for his "Arthuresque" novel *Méliador* and many poems.

Jean Froissart at his desk, writing his huge Chronicles. Jean Froissart's Chronicles, mid XVth century.
*(Bibliothèque d'Amiens Métropole, Ms 486 f° 001. Photograph CNRS-IRHT)*

The coronation of Charles V and his wife, Jeanne de Bourbon in 1364. Ornate "entrecolonnement" (intercolumn space), illuminated initial. Grandes Chroniques de France, circa 1380.
*(Bibl. mun. de Lyon, Ms P.A. 30 f° 418.*
*Photograph Bibliothèque municipale de Lyon, Didier Nicole).*

## The mad king

Charles V passed away on September 1380. He too, left a young son, also named Charles. In the shadow of the young prince, the merciless struggle for power began. His uncles, Louis d'Anjou, Jean de Berry and Philipp the Bold, the powerful Duke of Bourgogne, dominated the regency council and royal politics. Anjou, drawn away by a fanciful imaginary Napolitan crown, left the scene in 1382. Berry and above all Bourgogne, held the reins until 1388. Influenced by his young brother, Louis d'Orléans, the King pushed aside burdensome relatives, preferring instead the *Marmousets* who had been in the service of his father. Charles VI's first fit of madness (1392) allowed the

# The madness of king Charles

*HRISTINE DE PISAN was worried about the young monarch's health from 1394. Charles V's scrupulous biographer ended one of her poems with these melancholic verses.*

*"Se prions Dieu, de très humble courage*
*Que au bon Roy soit escu et deffense*
*Contre tous maulx, et de son grief malage*
*Lui doint santé; car j'ai ferme créance*
*Que, s'il avoit de son mal allégeance,*
*Encore seroit, quoiqu'adès en die,*
*Prince vaillant et de bonne ordonnance*
*Nostre bon Roy qui est en maladie."* [1]

_____

1. "So pray to God humbly and with all your heart. So that He will be a shield and protection to the good King against all evils and his serious illness. May he give him health, as I am convinced that if he vanquishes his illness, he will be, whatever might be said, a valiant prince and of wise government, our good ailing King."

Bold to regain power. His rivalry with Louis d'Orléans became more violent. Murder after murder was committed and plots were rife. Jean the Fearless took over from the Bold in 1404 and had Orleans assassinated on November 23, 1407. The later's son, Charles d'Orléans, carried the torch of paternal hatred, helped by his father in law, Bernard VII of Armagnac. The famous rivalry between Armagnacs and Bourguignons would leave a bloody trail throughout the kingdom for many long decades.

This was the moment that the English enemy chose to remember their continental claims. In 1399, Henry of Lancaster overthrew Richard II. According to his interests, he intervened from afar in France and the princes' quarrels. His son, Henry V, who came to the throne in 1413, went further still. He demanded that the terms of the old treaty of Bretigny be respected, claimed the rest of Jean the Good's ransom, as well as… Normandy! The weakness of the French monarchy and the general anarchy encouraged Henry to act militarily. He landed near the port of Harfleur with a strong army mid August 1415. Harfleur was taken after an epic siege that was immortalised by William Shakespeare. He then headed north towards Calais, in the great tradition of the lightning raids of the first part of the Hundred Years War. The French went in pursuit and caught up with him, for their sins, at Agincourt. In the evening of October 25, 1415, the Fren-

*Opposite.*
**Philipp the Good painted by Rogier van der Weyden school, oil on wood circa 1450.**
*(Photo: Hugo Maertens © Musée des Beaux-Arts de Dijon)*

*Below.* **The recumbent statue of Philipp the Bold. Palais des ducs de Bourgogne, Dijon.**

The equestrian statue of Du Guesclin by Arthur J. Le Duc (Caen).

# The routiers

 **UICKLY, the two sides, in order to reinforce their armies, recruited mercenaries or routiers.**

These professional soldiers, originally landless gentry, ruined peasants or bourgeois forced to the road by hunger, sold their services to the highest bidder. The Hundred Years War, however, did not keep them in continual service. During the long periods of truce, without pay or means, they roamed the countryside in search of sustenance.

After the treaty of Brétigny, the famous *Compagnies* desolated the kingdom of France. Charles V sent them to fight in the Castille against the Moors under the command of Du Guesclin. The infamous Ecorcheurs were rampant between 1430 and 1445. One of Charles VII's main tasks would be to rid the country of these wandering gangs that infested it.

**The pillaging of the town of Saint-Lô by Edward III's troops (1346). When the English landed in Normandy, no town was really capable of defending itself. The violence portrayed in the scene bears witness, however, to the necessity of solid walls. Jean Froissart's Chronicles, beginning of the XVth century.**
*(Bibl. mun. de Besançon, Ms 864 f° 130. picture CNRS-IRHT)*

11

ch dead lay in their thousands, whilst the English losses amounted to a handful. Two years later, Henry returned and began the all-out conquest of Normandy. The victor soon found himself in a position to demand exorbitant terms. After the humiliating treaty of Brétigny, France found itself under the drastic treaty of Troyes (1420). Charles VI, a mere puppet, remained a paper king. The Lancastrian married his daughter, Catherine, agreed to an alliance with the new Duke of Burgundy, Phillip the Good, and became regent of France and the next in line to the throne. Charles, the young heir apparent, eldest son of Charles VI, was simply removed from the line of succession.

## The final victory

The early death of Henry V (August 31, 1422) did not immediately change the order of things. His son, Henry VI, a baby of only a few months, succeeded him. Charles VI died shortly after on October 21, 1422 and the little Henry bore the burden of the English and French crowns under the regency of the famous Bedford. However, Charles, the heir apparent, had no intention of abdicating and had not given up on his claims. He also proclaimed himself king. He dominated *de facto* all of the country south of the Loire with the exception of the Guyenne. In the east he was threatened by the powerful state of Bourguignon. His position therefore looked to be shaky, even if he could count on the solid support of a loyal few and on a well structured territory. His army was heavily defeated at Verneuil-sur-Avre on

# Riots

**ERIODS OF GREAT MISERY always make for discontentment of the people. The terrible years that followed the military disasters were no exception to the rule.**

Crushing taxes, the ostentatious lifestyle of the Court, and growing instability in living conditions added to the collective fury. The great peasant Jacquerie of 1358 broke out at the same time as the Parisian riots lead by Étienne Marcel.

Moreover, the capital was shaken several times by violent events, such as the *Maillotins* revolt in 1382 and that of the *Cabochiens* in 1413. All the revolts were directly aimed at royal power or were part of the partisan struggles. The political reversals led, in general, to pitiless repressions.

The anonymous author of the *"Complaincte du povre Commun et des povres laboureurs de France"* was stirred into saying:
*"Gens d'armes et les trois Estatz
Qui vivez sur nous laboureurs [...]
Vin ne froment ne autre blé,
Pas seullement du pain d'avoine,
N'avons nostre saoul la moitié."* [1]

---

1. *"Warriors and the three states (probably referring to the nobles, clergy and bourgeoisie) that live off us, labourers... we don't have half of what we need in wine, wheat and other cereals, not even oat bread (normally used for feeding cattle)."*

*Opposite, left.*
**The heroine of an entire nation, Joan of Arc has been portrayed in many ways. Petite Jeanne d'Entrammes (Mayenne).** *(RR)*

*Following page.*
**Pierrefonds. Equestrian statue of Louis d'Orléans by Emmanuel Frémiet.**

August 17, 1424. In October 1428, the English laid siege to Orleans, the key to Charles' states. Things did not look good but the pieces were in place for the reconquest. All that was needed was the spark…

It came from the Lorraine, in the form of a young maiden. Joan found the *"Gentle Dauphin"* in Chinon (October 23, 1429), obtained a small army and left to lift the siege of Orleans under the amazed gaze of the great captains who thought they had seen everything (May 8). Immediately after, she crushed the enemy in a pitched battle at Patay (June 18) and had Charles crowned in the purest tradition of the French monarchy at Reims (July 17). The Valois now basked in a prestige that his rival could not aspire to. Victory had chosen its side, and nothing, not even Joan's burning at the stake in Rouen (May 30, 1431) could change the new order. Charles made his peace with the Duke of Burgundy in 1435 and was now free to take back his capital. His troops took the city on April 13, 1436. A Paris bourgeois who witnessed the events for himself, described the historic scene between two reflections on the price of wheat: *"the first to enter was the lord of Isle-Adam on a large scaling ladder which he climbed, placing the standard of France above the gate and exclaiming: The city is ours!"*

The king worked hard at reorganizing his lands. He set up the famous *compagnies d'ordonnance* (men at arms), predecessors of the permanent army, eradicated the last groups of routiers and made sure he had a regular fiscal income. He understood the advantage he could gain from new gunpowder weapons and employed the Bureau brothers in order to build up an efficient artillery arm. With the victory at Formigny (April 14, 1450) the gates to Normandy were opened. The battle of Castillon (July 17, 1453), at last gave him the Guyenne and ended 113 years of direct hostilities. Out of the whole kingdom of France, the English were left only with Calais.

The privilege of ending this century of hate fell to Louis XI. The peace treaty of Piquigny, signed along with king Edward IV in 1475, officially ended the conflict. The human and material toll was heavy on both sides. The more serious consequences, however, are no doubt found elsewhere. As Jacques le Goff rightly said, this long period of suffering affected above all the future by *"exacerbating the French and English nationalistic feelings and tainting them with xenophobia."*

# In the shelter of the fortresses

*Et par tant rendirent lesdittes fortresses,
ainsy que dit est, et s'en alèrent et partirent
environ L fuste de lanches et bien
IIIc communs de povres gens Du plat pais* [1]

anonymous chronicle from the reign of Charles VI

**OR THE MAJORITY** of the inhabitants of the good kingdom of France, the Hundred Years War began with a rumour: The *"Anglois"* had landed in Normandy and devastated many good lands, devastated some towns and villages and defeated the King at Crécy. Everyone was now aware that their precarious happiness could disappear in the wake of a savage horde, pillaging everything in its path, forcing themselves upon the women and cutting the throats of the men folk.

*Below.*
**The Tour de la Chaîne sits at the entrance of the port of La Rochelle.**

*Opposite.*
**The castle of Vitré.**

*1. "So they gave back the fortresses in the manner that had been agreed, left them and went on their way with around fifty lances and three hundred pitiful people from the surrounding countryside."*

14

# The great raid of 1346

**ROISSART WROTE with remarkable precision about the great chevauchée in the Cotentin lead by Edward III in 1346.**

Certain details are revealed that say a lot about the English strategy. The bourgeois of Barfleur preferred to surrender *"pour le doublance de mort"* [1]. Cherbourg was partially pillaged and burnt *"mès dedens le chastiel ne peurent il entrer, car il le trouvèrent trop fort et bien garni de gens d'armes."* [2] Carentan resisted to a lesser extent and the English *"fisent assaillir au dit chastiel par deux jours, si fortement qui cil qui dedens estoient et qui nul secours ne veoient, le rendirent, salve leurs corps et leur avoir."* [3] When it was impossible to hold on to the fortress *"si l'ardirent tout en abatirent"* [4], the instructions were clear: open the gates of a maximum number of towns in order to pillage them, take the weakly defended parts without seeking to hold on to them and evade in the face of heavy resistance.

---

1. *"By fear of death".*
2. *"But they could not enter the inside of the castle, as this was too well defended and served by warriors."*
3. *"They attacked the castle for two days and with such strength that those who were inside, seeing no help on the horizon, surrendered in return for their lives being spared and the promise of being able to keep their possessions."*
4. *"They burned it to the ground"*

*Above.*
**The castle of Montbrun.**
*(photo Didier Faure)*

*Following page, above.*
**Part of the town's walls at Avignon.**
*(Photo Yann Kervran)*

*Following page, below.*
**The castle of La Roche-Goyon.**

*Below, from left to right.* **King David in front of a fortress.**
**The palace towers have pepperbox roofs. Many wide windows have been set into the walls. The main tower has a nice ring of machicolations. Franciscan missal, end of the XVth century.**
*(Bibl. mun. de Lyon, Ms 514 f° 15 v°.*
*Photograph Bibliothèque municipale de Lyon, Didier Nicole.)*

**The fortress has been destroyed. This was the risk run by garrisons that put up too much of a fight. The victor was, in principal, merciless. Historiated initial. Franciscan missal, end of the XVth century.**
*(Bibl. mun. de Lyon, Ms 514 f° 17 v°. photograph*
*Bibliothèque municipale de Lyon, Didier Nicole.)*

## The "inheritance" of peace

People soon became used to a peace that they believed would last forever. Men at the beginning of the XIVth century were no exception to the rule. The minor lord had, for a long time, believed it no longer necessary to invest in the modernisation of his fortress; the city-dweller (for french medieval term *"bourgeois"*) thought it unnecessary to maintain the urban defences. What was the point in putting large amounts of money into military construction when it was no longer of any use? The order that had been established from the beginning of the reign of Phillip Auguste guaranteed a certain peace of mind, the spectre of private wars faded and nobody thought of a long violent conflict with another kingdom. Moreover, notably in the countryside, stone had progressively won over wood and earth as the main construction material and had put beyond the means of many the new techniques of fortification. The noblemen of the outermost bounds of the Berry or Normandy, admittedly, did not

build solid dwellings, but did they have the means to do so? Only
the great territorial princes had the resources necessary in order to
employ expensive specialists such as architects and masons.

## The cost of survival

Everything changed when war reared its head along with its trail
of atrocities. As Jean Favier said, *"War fell cruelly on thousands of
villages that would never see fighting but whose lord had no choice but to fortify his manor, at the expense of the yokel, and hundreds
of towns that were never besieged but which were dependant on the
defences. For a hundred years, this would be the single most expensive part of the budget."* To sum up, the survival of a small urban
or rural community depended on the quality of the walls that were
meant to protect it. This survival came at a price and everyone, at
their own level, had to pay for it. The different local authorities had
no qualms in bleeding dry the taxpayer or the serfs.

For the designated enemies, at the beginning of the conflict, did
not try to attack the strongholds. The raising of an army and its
upkeep was very expensive. They could not, therefore, allow themselves to become bogged down in a long siege that eroded the moral
of the troops and uselessly wasted finances whilst often ending with
mixed results. A handful of warriors protected behind solid defences
was potentially capable of keeping at bay a large number of troops
for many weeks. King Jean the Good found this out for himself at
Breteuil (Eure) from mid July to mid August 1356. As well as this,
once a fortress was taken, they would have to hold on to it and there were thousands in France. Garrisons were a drain on budgets.

The English were not averse to the occasional pillaging of a city
when it could be taken with ease, as was the case, notably with Caen
in 1346. They did, however, generally avoid areas that were too well
defended, preferring to devastate the vulnerable countryside taking
off with the spoils and when possible fight their enemies in the open.
All of the great raids of the Hundred Years War used this tactic with
the exception of the conquest of Normandy by Henry V from 1417

## ħenry V and ɲormandy

**ENRY V OF LANCASTER,** *during
the year 1417, broke with his
predecessors' tactics. The army that
had landed at Trouville on August 1,
1417, would no longer go on a great
chevauchée but would begin
the all out conquest of Normandy.*

Caen, Alençon, Argentan and Cherbourg fell after a siege. Falaise and Evreux suffered the same fate. Rouen finally opened its gates to the King on January 20, 1419.
The burgess of Paris wrote thus about the events: *"Item, le 20ᵉ jour de janvier, audit
an 1419, entrèrent les Anglais dedans Rouen, et la gagnèrent par leur force."* [1] Normandy had therefore fallen after a brave fight. Witnesses of the English desire to settle long term, the people of Caen, like those of Harfleur in 1415, were made to leave,
with people arriving from England and settling in the abandoned houses.

*1. "On the twentieth day of January in the year of our Lord, 1419. The English entered
Rouen and took it by force".*

19

# The frontier of Calais

**ONCE THIS** *important town was in English hands (1347), the French began fortifying the surrounding area.*

Small castles, villages, churches and abbeys all served to make a network capable of housing small armed groups or act as look out posts. It was, on the other hand, out of the question to stop the larger raids with such weak constructions.

to 1419. The wall, for the locals, was a deterrent! Therefore many a peasant watched his farm burn from the castle ramparts behind which he had taken refuge in order to save his life. The attackers passed in the distance but the loss of crops condemned the survivors to inescapable starvation shortly afterwards.

### The soudards *(rough soldiers)*

In the eyes of the rural populations, the main scourge generated by the conflict was, no doubt, that of the wandering groups of pillaging soldiers. We have already mentioned here the *Grandes Compagnies* who laid waste the country after the treaty of Brétigny, or the Ecorcheurs who were rife at the beginning of the reign of Charles VII. Like the English, these men did not like to spend too much time in the same place. When there were too many, the fear they provoked often lead wealthy towns in their path to pay them to leave. When they swarmed in undisciplined gangs, they had a free hand to lay waste vast areas. It was in this atmosphere of double threat that many fortresses seem to have been built or modernised. These were often made up of a donjon of varying size and shape with a relatively small enceinte. To this series of constructions can be added, for example, Polignac (Haute-Loire), Septmonts (Aisne), Vez (Oise), Crouy-sur-Ourcq (Seine-et-Marne), Largöet-en Elven (Morbihan) and Tancarville (Seine-Maritime). Jean Mesqui said that *"these constructions that rose above the countryside were no doubt enough to keep away most of the routiers on the look out for plunder; the tower was a symbol of power."*

Sometimes even old earth ramparts were re-used. Digs at Fontenois-les-Montbozon (Haute-Saône) at the place named Chastel de Messire Girard, have revealed two periods of occupation on the site. The date of the first remains undetermined (XIth or XIIth centuries?). The second, on the other hand, is better known thanks to what was found. This included coins from the second half of the XIVth century, a crossbow bolt and even part of a horn used for raising the alarm. Eric Affolter and Jean-Claude Voisin, the archaeologists in charge of the dig, emphasize the surprising coincidence between this phase of temporary colonisation and the reporting of companies of routiers in the area. This example of an abandoned primitive stronghold being re-used is no doubt not the only one, but there is a lack of information in this field. It does, however, say a lot about the chronic insecurity of those troubled times.

### The "Brigand's castle"

The fortress was a godsend for a horde of outlaws that managed to take it. It allowed them to lay waste a large area then return with their plunder which was safe in the shelter of the towers and curtain

*Above, right.*
**The castle and medieval village of Curemonte.**
*Opposite.*
**The fortress of Largoët-en-Elven.**
*(Photo Cyrille Castellant)*

*Following page, bottom.*
**The keep of Polignac culminates on a rocky dyke, projecting its power over the surrounding lands.**

*Opposite.*
**The formidable keep of Septmonts dominates a palatial complex dating from the XIVth century that was built for the comfort of the bishops of Soissons.**

*Following page.*
**Château de Rochebaron.**

walls. This way of operating was by no means new. The Vikings used the same methods from the safety of their famous Jeufosse hideaway. Robert Guiscard did the same, sheltered by the motte of San Marco Argentano in Italy. During the Hundred Years War, this phenomenon happened regularly all over the country. In Froissart's writings, this resulted in several acts of bravery. He related the use of Ventadour by the redoubtable Geoffroy Black Head (Tête-Noire): *"Ce Joffroy Teste Noire et ses gens tindrent Ventadour, par lequel ilz adommagièrent moult le pays et prindrent plusieurs fors chasteaux en Auvergne, en Roergue, en Limosin, en Quersin, en Chevaldam, en Bigorre et en Agenois, tout venant l'un de l'autre."* [2] Peasants and minor lords from these areas would no doubt remember for a very long time, at least those who survived, the pillaging activities of Geoffroy and his disreputable companions.

## The military role of the castle according to Charles V

The wise King, as we know, was hardly partial to the great *chevauchées* punctuated by risky battles. Still smarting from the disasters of Crécy and Poitiers, the King totally broke from the strategy, if there had been one, of his predecessors. He ordered his captains to systematically avoid any confrontation in the open country. On July 19, 1367, he promulgated an edict on fortifications, ordering every lord and town to reinforce the ramparts. All of these towns and strong points had to have supplies, weapons, munitions and enough men. Those who did not have the means to obey the royal edicts were forced to demolish their defences. The enemy could not, at any price, take control of any strong point. The experience of what happened at Saint-Sauveur-le-Vicomte (Manche) was a painful reminder. The

*(Continued on page 26)*

---

2. *"This Geoffroi Tete-Noire* (Black Head) *and his men took Ventadour and from there pillaged the entire region and took several other castles in the Auvergne, Rouergue, Limousin, Quercy, Gévaudan, Bigorre and in Agenois, ceaselessly going from one to the other."*

# The "Très Riches Heures du duc de Berry"

*EAN DE BERRY (1340-1416), the brother of Charles V, played a considerable political role during his nephew's, King Charles VI's, minority, and the years of turmoil that followed the disclosure of his mental illness.*

He was also known for his taste for splendour and luxury. An enlightened patron, he supported a string of artists: architects, sculptors, painters, illuminators…

One of his manuscripts made up of his immense collection, the *"Très Riches Heures"*, gives a remarkable insight into several fortress-palaces of his time. Against an ultramarine sky in the background of every day scenes, can be seen the outlines of the Louvre, Lusignan, Dourdan, Etampes, Saumur, Vincennes or Poitiers.

A forgotten world comes to life in a blaze of shimmering colours and unusual forms. The characters seem to come to life. An absolute masterpiece!

**Under a canopy, duc Jean de Berry prays to saint André.**
**Evangéliaire attributed to the Pseudo-Jacquemart de Hesdin, circa 1405**
*(Bibl. mun. de Bourges, Ms 48 f° 181. photo CNRS-IRHT)*

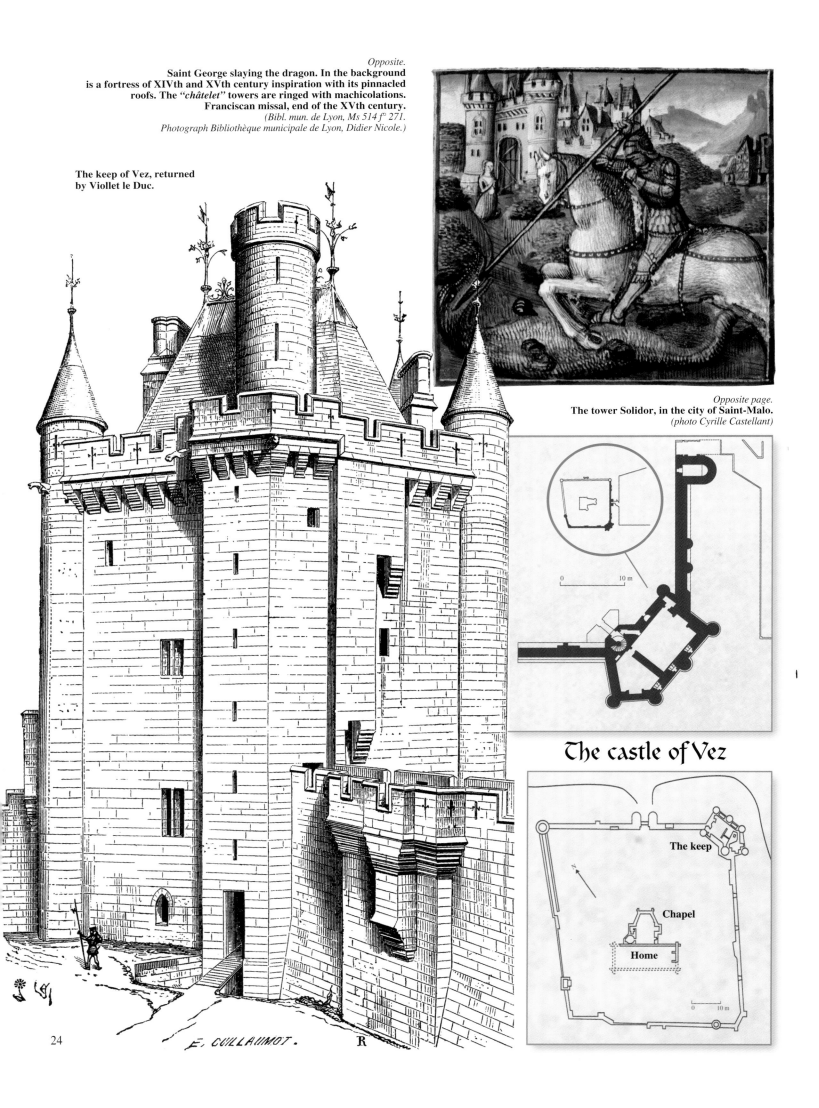

*Opposite.*
**Saint George slaying the dragon. In the background
is a fortress of XIVth and XVth century inspiration with its pinnacled
roofs. The *"châtelet"* towers are ringed with machicolations.
Franciscan missal, end of the XVth century.**
*(Bibl. mun. de Lyon, Ms 514 f° 271.*
*Photograph Bibliothèque municipale de Lyon, Didier Nicole.)*

**The keep of Vez, returned
by Viollet le Duc.**

*Opposite page.*
**The tower Solidor, in the city of Saint-Malo.**
*(photo Cyrille Castellant)*

0          10 m

# The castle of Vez

**The keep**

**Chapel**

**Home**

0      10 m

E. GUILLAUMOT.

*Above.*
**Fortress of Foix.**

*Opposite.* **Castle of Saint-Sauveur-le-Comte.**

*Double following page.*
**The fortress palace of Saumur, built on a XIIIth century base by Louis I^er d'Anjou at the end of the XIVth century.**

*(Continued from page 22)*

opposing side that held the castle reigned with terror over the surrounding countryside for many years. The tactic of Charles V began to show results. The English now roamed throughout a deserted country, looking in vain to fight the French encamped behind their walls. The latter did not hesitate in attacking the enemy in the rear, cutting off supplies and exterminating stray troops. The meagre spoils taken by the invader were the final straw in breaking their moral. They began to withdraw.

Charles now moved to the offensive and patiently re-conquered what had been given away at Brétigny. On all fronts, his armies began by taking the strong points in strategic places: crossroads, ports, bridges… Certain garrisons that resisted strongly were quite simply paid to leave. Captain Chatterton accepted to leave Saint-Sauveur-le-Vicomte in this way, receiving 50,000 francs in 1375. The advance was also quick in the Aquitaine. The remaining pockets, made up of dozens of small stubborn strong points, would be dealt with later. In this context, the castle returned fully to its initial, ancestral use; that of controlling the land. The taking of a castle meant the total control over the surrounding countryside. The King also knew how to preserve the benefits the victories had brought, as Christine de Pisan said: *"Je ne trouve en chronique, n'escrips, ne personne qui me le die, que chose conquise, fust cité, terre, fortresse, ou autre besoigne, onques puis, en son temps fust perdue par rebellacion, ne autrement; qui est chose merveilleuse et hors le commun cours des choses conquises à l'espée, qui souvent se seulent rebeller et entregecter en divers*

 *(Continued on page 32)*

# Gaston III de Foix

**A PRINCE OF IMMENSE wealth, Gaston Fébus (1331-1391) is above all known for his fabulous "Livre de la chasse" (Book of hunting), an illuminated gem and precious insight into the way the court lived in a bygone age.**

He managed to remain almost independent from the crown of Valois and kept himself out of the Anglo-French conflict. A neighbour to the Navarre and the Aragon, he very quickly employed the architect, Sicard de Lordat, giving him the task of making unassailable strong holds for his states. This led to the creation or restoration of Mauvezin (Hautes-Pyrénées), Pau, Montaner and perhaps Orthez (Pyrénées-Atlantiques). In this way, he intended to prevent any possible incursions into all of his territories and assert his power.

**Gaston Fébus and his huntsmen.**
**The princes of the Hundred Years War period liked to live in incredible luxury. The Hunting Book of Gaston Fébus, beginning of the XVth century.**
*(Paris, Bibl. nat. de France Ms. Fr. 616 f° 13)*

*Opposite. "Febus me fe"* **(Fébus made me). The terse inscription above the count of Foix coat of arms leaves no doubts as to the identity of the man who had the castle of Montaner built.**
*(photo William Gondoin)*

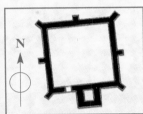

*Below.*
**The fortress of Mauvezin, built by Gaston Fébus.**
*(photo château de Mauvezin)*

# The Ecorcheurs

**ITEM, A L'ENTRÉE DE JUILLET** vint une grant compaignie de larrons et de murdriers qui se logerent ès villaiges qui sont au tour de Paris, et tellement jusques à six ou environ huit lieues de Paris, homme n'osoit aller aux champs [...]

*Ne fust moyne, prestre, ne religieux de quelque ordre, fust nonnain, ménestrel, héraut, fust femme ou enffant de quelque âge, que s'il yssoit dehors Paris qui ne fust en grand péril de sa vie ; mais se on ne lui ostoit sa vie, il estoit despouillé tout nû tous sans ung seul excepter, de quelque estat qu'il fust ; et quand on s'en plaignoit aux gouverneurs de Paris, ils respondoient : Il faut qu'ils vivent, le Roy y mettra*

**The rebuilding of the castle of Sully-sur-Loire by Viollet-le-Duc in the XIXth century.**

*bien bref remede. Et de cette compaignie estoient principalement Pierre Regnault, Floquart, Lextrac et plusieurs autres, tous membres d'Antecrist, car tous estoient larrons et murdriers, boute-feux, efforceurs de touttes femmes, et leurs compaignies."* [1]

"Journal d'un Bourgeois de Paris" year 1444.
*Hors les murailles, point de salut.*

*1. "Likewise, at the beginning of the month of July, a large group of thieves and murderers settled in the villages around Paris. In a perimeter of six or seven leagues, no man dared to go to the fields... There was neither monk, nor priest or any kind of religious person, no nun, craftsman or messenger, woman or child regardless of age, who did not risk his life if he happened to leave Paris. If they were not killed they were thoroughly robbed, whatever their rank. When complaints were made to the authorities in Paris, they answered: They have to live; the King will put an end to it. Pierre Regnault, Floquet, Lestrac and several others, were the chiefs of this terrible company. They were nothing but thieves, murderers, arsonists and rapists."*

*Above and below.* **Two views of the very elegant castle of Sully-sur-Loire and its moats**

*Opposite, from top to bottom.*
**Philippe Auguste lays siege to the town of Aumale.**
**The scene is supposed to take place circa 1200.**
**The fortress, however, is typical of a XIVth century construction.**
**This can be seen in the corner towers with their corbels.**
**Grandes Chroniques de France, circa 1350.**
**Polylobed frame, ornate initials,**
*(Bibl. mun. de Lyon, Ms 880 f° 262.*
*Photograph Bibliothèque municipale de Lyon, Didier Nicole.)*

**The plan of the castle of Pau.**

**Montsoreau, built in the middle of the XVth century**
**by an acquaintance of Charles VII.**

*Following page.*
**Mehun-sur-Yèvre, entirely modified**
**at the end of the XIVth century for duc Jean de Berry.**

*(Continued from page 26)*

*mains; mais, si bonnes garnisons, si loyales et si propres furent mises és terres et fortreces, que, Dieu merci, furent tenues et demourent en leur estat."* [3]

## A living space

We should be wary of limiting the castle in the years between 1350 and 1450 to a purely military role. For the mighty, it was above all a living environment in perfect harmony with the period's princely way of life. It had, of course, to allow for defence in times of crisis but also the lavish ways of a large court, fond of their entertainment. All this time, the peasant died of hunger in his ravaged fields, whilst the indifferent noblemen lived a life of pleasure and led a life of expensive debauchery. The old, austere fortifications were transformed into magnificent residences. Charles V instigated the fashion by totally transforming the Louvre. Commanded by the architect, Raymond du Temple, masons, carpenters, stone cutters, painters, sculptors and cabinet makers combined ingenuity and talent to offer their master a setting that befitted him.

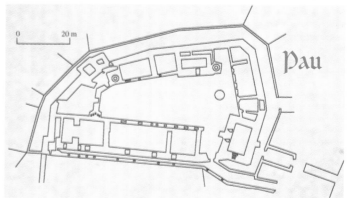

As in the time of Phillip Auguste, the Louvre once more inspired the creatively minded. The princes of *"fleur-de-lis"*, Louis of Anjou, Jean of Berry and Phillip of Burgondy, paid fortunes to secure the services of the disciples of Raymond du Temple. Spurred on by the royal family, the great territorial lords thought of only one thing, to beautify their residences: the counts of Brittany, Foix or Savoie among others, started impressive building programmes. The important restoration work at Coucy was also started at this time.

Fortresses now vied with each other in aesthetics and beauty, vertical paintings asserted the sophisticated tastes and power of their owners. We won't go so far as to say that the work on the Louvre or Saumur contained the seed that lead to Chambord or Azay-le-Rideau, but in many ways, the work carried out heralded the Renaissance. This pursuit of comfort and magnificence also touched the countryside and more modest residences. The country squire liked to think that he could live like the mighty of the world.

The period of 1350-1450 was, for the most part, affected by a renewed need to shelter behind solid fortifications, as is the case in all periods of great insecurity. The contemporary lord of the Hundred Years War hardly differed in this way, from the Gallo-roman *dominus* (master), confronted for the first time by a horde of Franks, or the Carolingian *comes* (count), contemplating fearfully a plundering group of Vikings. Can the more recent great forts of Vauban, those of 1870 and the Maginot Line be seen as the re-occurring result of a natural and ancestral reflex?

3. *"I can find nothing, be it written or chronicled, no one can tell me of anything he has conquered, town, land, fortress or any other thing, that was lost in his time to revolt or anything else. This is astonishing and unusual for things that have been conquered by the sword often turn to revolt and throw themselves in other hands. The garrisons he placed in conquered lands and fortresses were so good, loyal and honest that, God be thanked, they were held and remained as they were."*

# La folie des grandeurs

*"Delusions of grandeur"*

Nostre roy Charles fust sage artiste,
Se démonstra vray architecteur,
deviseur certain et prudent ordeneur,
lorsque les belles fondacions fist faire en maintes places,
notables édifices beaulx et nobles,
tant d'esglises comme de chasteauls et austres bastimens,
à Paris et ailleurs.[1]

Christine de Pisan

**THE MOVEMENT that had begun during the XIIIth century was confirmed. The castle remained, of course, a place that was protected from the outside world, but this place had, above all, to provide the level of comfort expected by the people who lived in it.**

It was no longer enough, for the great of this world, to live spartanly in cold and badly lit dwellings. It was time now for long pointed shoes, jewels, pelisse and hennins (horned head dress), all within the walls of fortresses-palaces and the setting of the escapades of a sumptuous and turbulent court.

(Continued on page 38)

1. *"Our king, Charles, was a wise artist. He proved to be a veritable architect, a prudent and wise organizer, when he made, in so many places, such beautiful and noble buildings, churches as well as castles and other buildings, in Paris and in other places."*

*Previous page, far left.* **The Virgin gives communion to Saint Avoie. The scene takes place in the XVth century castle-palace with its high pepper-box roofed towers, mullion windows and canonniers. The book of hours, circa 1425.**
*(Bibl. mun. de Lyon, Ms 5140 f° 70. Photograph Bibliothèque municipale de Lyon, Didier Nicole.)*

*Previous page, centre from top to bottom.* **The decoration receives particular attention. Château de Montsoreau. The fireplace once heated the great hall of the palace of Chinon.**

*Above.* **The huge fortress of Clisson.**

*Below.*
**The keep of the castle of Vincennes is placed in a square enceinte, isolated from the rest of the fortress by a deep dry moat.**
*(Photograph Cyrille Castellant)*

35

*The Pope of Aquitaine origin, Clement V, decided, after his election in 1305, not to settle in Rome, a city plagued by quarrels between rival political factions.*

He chose the town of Avignon, situated on the lands of the Germanic empire, but only separated from the French kingdom by the river Rhône. The throne of Saint Peter also owned, close by, an important estate, the Comtat Venaissin. Jean XXII, was content, after Clement V, to restore the old Pope's palace where he resided. It was Benedict XII who, from 1335, started the project of an enormous fortified complex that was to protect and house the pontifical Curia. Work began under the command of the master, Pierre Poisson. Clement VI, entrusted the task of enlarging and beautifying his predecessor's project, to the architect Pierre de Loubières. The town was also closed off by an enormous enceinte. The times would turn out to be difficult ones and these pre-cautions were not without use but they did not put every ones mind at rest. Innocent VI preferred to pay off the routiers of Arnaud de Cervole that were marauding in the region, with 20,000 gold florins, rather than suffer a full-scale siege. The Popes definitively moved back to Rome under the initiative of Gregory IX (1362-1370).

**The Pope's palace at Avignon. The main gate has a recess bearing the papal coat of arms.** *(Photos Yann Kervran)*

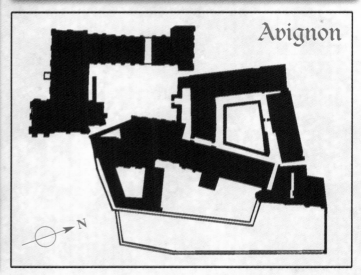

Avignon

*(Continued from page 34)*

## The first sites

So once more the example came from the French monarchy. As in the old days, Phillip Auguste had progressively imposed his architectural models throughout his kingdom, Charles V was a role model to those of his subjects rich enough to copy him. A huge yards, under the command of the architect, Raymond du Temple, was begun at the Louvre in the last part of the XIVth century. It was perhaps partly inspired by the splendid Palace of the Popes built in Avignon, mostly under the ponti-

**The Louvre at the time of Charles V restored by Viollet le Duc.**

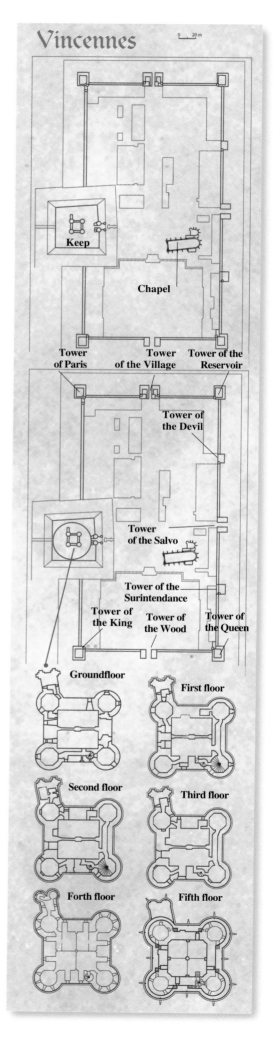

### Vincennes

0   20 m

Keep

Chapel

Tower of Paris

Tower of the Village

Tower of the Reservoir

Tower of the Devil

Tower of the Salvo

Tower of the Surintendance

Tower of the King

Tower of the Wood

Tower of the Queen

Groundfloor

First floor

Second floor

Third floor

Forth floor

Fifth floor

Tower of the Village, one of the castle of Vincennes' large gate towers that were used as residences.
*(Photograph Cyrille Castellant)*

*Above.* **Château d'Angers. The palace's gatehouse and chapel (XIVth – XVth centuries).**

*Opposite, on the right and from top to bottom.*
**The fortress of Clisson is well protected by a barbican.**

**The fortress of Blandy-les-Tours.**
*(Photo Cyrille Castellant)*

*Following page.*
**The fortress of Bourbon l'Archambault, was deeply transformed by Dukes of Bourbon at the eve of XVth century.**
*(Office de Tourisme et de Thermalisme de Bourbon-l'Archambault et sa Région)*

ficates of Benedict XII (1334-1342) and Clement VI (1342-1352). The latter, especially, did not hold back when it came to setting out the sumptuous interior. The Garde-Robe tower, with its bathroom, bedroom and murals was a marvellous example. The centuries may have spared the Palace of the Popes but nothing exists of the Louvre today. There is, however, an almost contemporary pictorial account of the finished site. This is the beautiful illumination of the month of October by the Limbourg brothers, in the famous *Très riches Heures du Duc de Berry*. All of the corner towers are seen with two added floors with pinnacles. High, pointed chimneys pierce the roofs. Golden pinnacles, turrets and watchtowers stand out against an azure sky. The curtain walls have been made higher and pierced with many wide mullions windows. Builders were now seemingly obsessed with light and aesthetics. The coming decades would reinforce this trend.

The austere construction, desired by Phillip Auguste nearly two hundred years before, that stone monster that ostensibly embodied the firmness of royal power, now became a magnificent fortified residence with large apartments of unheard-of luxury. Charles V, a book connoisseur, even installed a library in the donjon that, in years gone by, dominated all the strongholds in the kingdom of France. This was the embryonic *Bibliothèque Nationale de France*.

The Valois did not stop there. A frenzied builder, he continued the construction of Vincennes until 1373, which had been started by his grandfather, Philip VI. A vast enceinte, 330 by 175 metres,

 *(Continued on page 46)*

*At the top.*
**The tour de Bar at Dijon.**

*Opposite.*
**The recumbent statue
of Philippe the Bold
in front of a richly decorated
monumental fireplace.
The palace of the dukes
of Burgundy, Dijon.**

*Following page at the top.*
**The apartments of Laval
are overlooked by a large
XIIIth century cylindrical tower
with a ring of hoardings**

*Following page below and below.*
**The royal apartments at Loches
and its great hall with
monumental fireplace.**

The Ponts-de-Cé, a well liked residence of king René d'Anjou.

**Like many old fortresses, Rochebaron underwent important modifications in the XIVth and XVth centuries.** *(photo Yann Kervran)*

# Mastering the light

*ROM NOW on, nobody hesitated to pierce through towers and curtain walls so that the soothing warmth of the sun could get through.*

**Window of the great hall at the castle of Angers.**

**Single lattice window, castle of Montsoreau**

The traditional twin bay windows were progressively replaced by beautiful mullion and lattice windows that sprung up all over the place. These were protected by iron grills to prevent anyone from entering from the outside. The use of glass became more commonplace. Wooden vantails, built on an interior fixed wooden frame, kept prying eyes away when necessary. These windows also had a strong symbolic connotation, revealing the status of the person who ordered the building. A double lattice window with six openings designated a person of royal blood (the King himself or a close relative). A single lattice (only four openings), on the other hand, designated a person of inferior rank.

**Single lattice window, castle of Saumur.**

45

*Above.*
**The squat castle of Saint-Mesmin,
overlooks the deep moats.**

*Following page.*
**Saumur: A XIVth century construction was built over foundations
probably dating from the time of Philippe Auguste.**

*(Continued from page 40)*

was flanked by nine rectangular towers. The towers of the Wood,
Salvo and Village, placed respectively on the southern, eastern and
northern flanks, allowed one to enter the fortress and acted as gate
towers. Within these were independent lodgings reserved for those
close to the royal power. Everything had been thought of for the
comfort of those who dwelled there. Wide bay windows let in plen-
ty of light, big fireplaces heated the large rooms, bedrooms, latrines…
At the heart of the court, the Sainte-Chapelle had pride of place, this
had been started at the end of the XIVth century and was finished
two centuries later.

The western curtain wall is interrupted by an autonomous enceinte that formed a perfect 50 metres sided square. In the centre is the
royal donjon that rises to the prodigious height of 52 metres. Also
square in shape, it has large, jutting out cylinders on its corners. Its
designers equipped it with a latrines tower, making an appendage
to the northwest turret. Each floor has ribbed arches. The ribs start
from a central pillar, join the keystone and finish at finely crafted
bases. The sovereign occupied the second floor which was well lit
and heated. Vincennes was the symbol of his authority and was supposed to master the common people.

Christine de Pisan mentioned the great list of Charles V's other
achievements, all, according to her, more impressive than the last.
These include Melun, Fontainebleau and Saint-Germain (Yvelines),
Creil and Compiègne (Oise) or the aptly named manoir de Beauté
(Val de Marne) and the hotel de Saint-Pol in Paris. In a strange twist
of fate that shows the futility of human endeavour and the fleeting
vanity of the powerful, none of these splendours, apart from Vincennes, has survived the passage of time.

## The school of Raymond du Temple

The princes of the "lys" and their biggest vassals, as we have seen,

# Getting about

***ALACES GREW TALLER. Stairs,
therefore, had to be made in order
to reach the upper floors, symbolically
leading the visitor up towards
the lofty spheres of power.***

Two distinct types can be seen from the beginning of the XIVth century, stairs with large steps and the large external spiral staircase.

The first usually go along the walls or are more rarely perpendicu-
lar to them. The steps lead out to a perron, a prestigious place from
which the Lord of the castle could greet his guests. It was also from such a place that he would speak to the crowds below. A perfect example has sur-
vived at Brancion.

The second tended
to take over from the
large steps in the
second half of the
XIVth century.

These soon spread,
based on the model of
the large spiral stair-
case at the Louvre,
famous throughout the
Kingdom in its day for
the richness of its
decoration; this sadly
has not survived.
However, there are
still some magnificent
examples at Saumur
or again Tarascon.

**Spiral staircase.
Castle of
Montsoreau.**

*Opposite.*
**Both within their respective towns, the castles of Annecy**
*(page 49)* **and of Chambéry** *(page 48)*
**show the strength of the Savoy House.**
*(photographs Emmanuel Naud)*

did not want to be outdone. Jean de Berry, the brother of Charles V, employed the services of Raymond's disciples, the brothers Drouet and Gui de Dammartin. Under the compass points and the rule of the masters, castle palaces were built in Bourges, Concressault or Mehun-sur-Yèvre (Cher), Lusignana or Poitiers (Vienne), Nonette and Riom (Puy-de-Dome). The House of Burgundy regularly poached the architects working for de Berry, rivalling in splendour at Dijon, Brancion (Saône-et Loire) or Hesdin (Pas-de-Calais). The Anjou renovated Angers and completely rebuilt Saumur, the Ponts-de-Cè (Maine-et-Loire) and Tarascon (Bouches-du-Rhône). Louis d'Orléans, the brother of King Charles VI, also began a series of immense projects on his lands of the Valois. Dying prematurely in 1407, he 'only' left us Pierrefonds (Oise), heavily overhauled in the XIXth century by Eugène Viollet-le-Duc, and the gigantic front of Ferté-Milon (Aisne). Several years later, in Chinon, the *"Gentle Dauphin"* Charles, the contested successor to the kingdom of France, had also built a main building befitting his rank. The site chosen was no doubt not politically insignificant. It was a stone's throw away from the chapel where the legendary ancestor of the kings of England, Henry Plantagenet, had passed away more than two hundred years before. Of the great hall, where, as legend has it, Joan of Arc famously met Charles, nothing remains today apart from a gable and a fireplace standing alone. Time has, however, spared most of the residential buildings. Although the embers no longer glow in the hearths, the mullion windows with their benches, on the other hand, still offer wonderful views over the peacefully flowing river Vienne. How many noble ladies, dressed in their finest attire, sat on these stone benches, so that they could, six centuries earlier, look out across the same countryside?

The territorial princes followed suit. The Dukes of Brittany transformed Suscinio and Vannes (Morbihan), the Counts of Savoy, Chambery and Annecy (Haute-Savoie) and those of Alençon their eponymous fortress. The lords of Bourbon did the same thing at Bourbon-Archambault, Hérisson and Billy (Allier).

Barons of lower rank, such as Enguerrand VII of Coucy (Aisne), the last in a proud line, also began the renovation of their properties. The new great hall of the Worthies of Coucy was inaugurated with great ceremony in the course of 1387. A wind of modernity blew throughout the kingdom and its provincial satellites. Old fortresses were progressively transformed to the architectural fashions. These included, Clisson (Loire-Atlantique), Vitré, Fougères, Montmuran (Ille-et-Villaine), Sully (Loiret), Laval (Mayenne), Lavardin (Loir-et-Cher) and Blandy-les-Tours (Seine-et-Marne). Lords of lesser importance, when they had the means to, tried to replicate in miniature the way of life of their superiors. Building went on at Saint-Mesmin (Deux-Sèvres), Saint-Sauveur-le-Vicomte (Manche), Oudon (Loire-Atlantique), Largöet-en-Elven, La Hunaudaye (Côtes-d'Armor), Sarzay (Indre) and Septmonts (Aisne). In most cases, we will come back to this, the residential donjon inspired by Vincennes, made a strong comeback. All of these castles, new or restored, now conformed to constraints imposed by the way of life of the period.

# Chinon

*The gigantic fortress is set on a rocky spur, that the riverbed of the Vienne follows for a good hundred metres. It is in three parts and is spread over more than 400 metres.*

*Opposite and above.*
**The XVth century apartments of the castle of Chinon.**

*Opposite page.*
**Machicolations with triple lobed motifs. The clock tower of the castle of Chinon.**

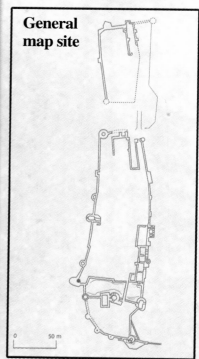

**General map site**

0    50 m

The clock tower of the castle of Chinon
(XIVth century).

52

*Above.*
**The slender silhouette of the castle of Chinon overlooking the peaceful waters of the Vienne.**

*Opposite.*
**The site of the great hall of the castle of Chinon. It was on the first floor. It was here that Charles VII first met Joan of Arc.**

The Saint-Georges fortress dominates the east, that of the Milieu the centre and finally, the Coudray fortress the west. The history of the site probably begins in the Bronze Age. Impregnable, it soon became a refuge to a community that was conscious of the advantages to be gained from such a position. Abandoned during the Roman period of peace, it was once more occupied at the time of the Germanic invasions. A castrum suffered a siege in the Vth century and the place was fortified by the counts of Blois towards the middle of the Xth century.

The Comte d'Anjou Geoffroi Martel took it in 1044 along with the rest of the Touraine. Henry II Plantagenet died in the castle's chapel on July 6, 1189. Phillip Auguste took it in a fierce battle after a long siege, in 1205. An utterly modified Chinon, then became a royal seat and because of this, held many state prisoners. The Phillip August tower at Coudray held several dignitaries of the Knights Templar after the wave of arrests in 1307. They left there mysterious inscriptions that have been pored over by countless thrill-seeking experts. It is also the place where Joan of Arc waited for several weeks before being granted an audience by the *"King of Bourges"*.

It was Phillip de Commines, Louis XI's right hand man, who was the last to leave his mark on the countlessly modified ancient walls, by adding the Tour d'Argenton in the last quarter of the XVth century.

*Following page at the top and below.*
**Like many other old fortresses, Rochebaron underwent many important modifications in the XIVth and XVth centuries.**

*Below and at the bottom.*
**Suscinio was completely overhauled by the last dukes of Brittany. There are sculpted heraldic motifs above the door.**

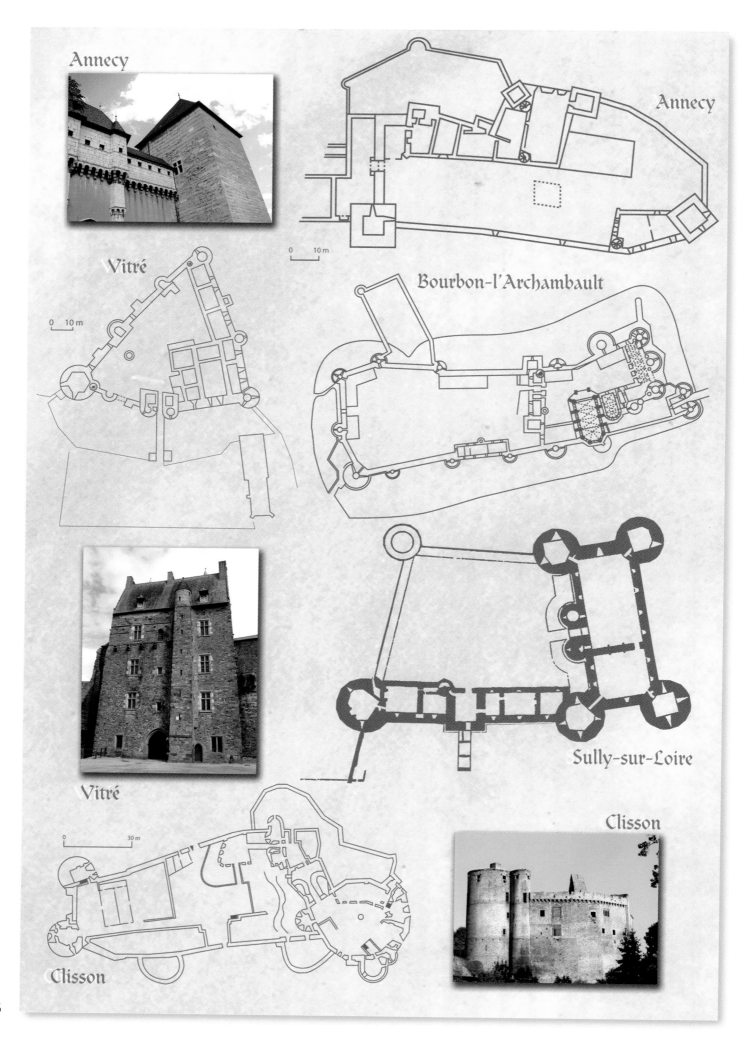

Annecy

Annecy

Vitré

Bourbon-l'Archambault

Sully-sur-Loire

Vitré

Clisson

Clisson

56

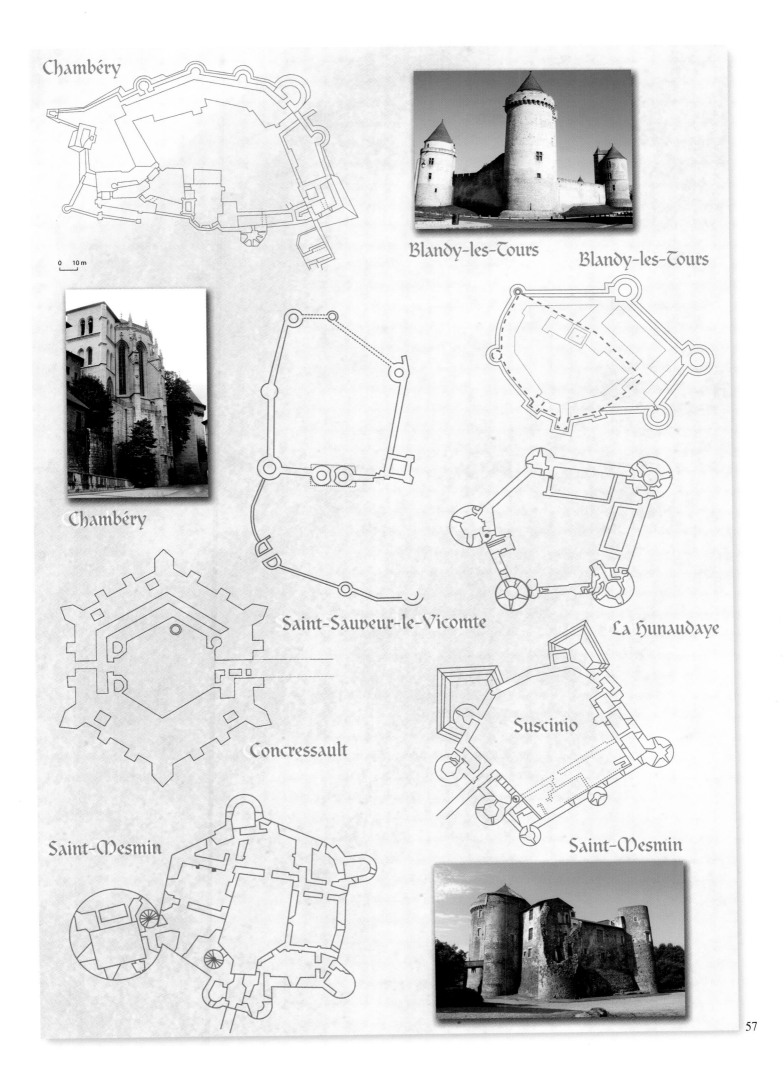

Chambéry

0 10 m

Blandy-les-Tours

Blandy-les-Tours

Chambéry

Saint-Sauveur-le-Vicomte

La Hunaudaye

Concressault

Suscinio

Saint-Mesmin

Saint-Mesmin

*Above.* **Jean Froissart at the court of Gaston Febus.**
**Jean Froissart's Chronicles, beginning of the XVth century.**
*(Bibl. mun. de Besançon, Ms 865 f° 201. Photo CNRS-IRHT)*

*Opposite.* **The keep at Montaner, built by the architect
Sicard Lordat for Gaston Fébus.** *(Photo William Gondoin)*

*Following page.* **Castle of Foix.**
*(Photo William Gondoin)*

## The lights of the court

This period, for those who did not die of hunger, was one of banquets, endless festivities only interrupted by hunting or minor fighting expeditions. Jean Froissart, the incomparable chronicler and tireless traveller, saw with his own eyes the luxurious life of the lord. He wrote with the amazement of a child at how he was received into Gaston Fébus' court. "*Quant de sa chambre à my-nuit venoit pour souper en sa salle, devant luy avoit douze torches allumées que douze varlets portoient, et icelles douze torces tenues estoient devant sa table, qui donnoient grant clareté en la salle, laquelle salle estoit pleine de chevalliers et escuiers, et tousjours estoient là à foison tables dreschiées pour souper, qui souper vouloit. Nuls ne parloit à luy à sa table, se il ne l'appelloit. Il mangeoit par coustume foison, vollaille, et en espécial les elles et les cuisses tant seulement; et lendemain au disner petit buvoit et mengeoit. Souvent il prendoit grant*

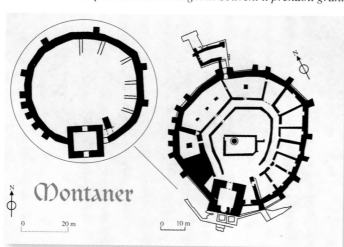

*Above and opposite.*
**The south wall of the great hall at the castle of Angers, with its mullion and lattice bay windows and its access in the middle of a norman Style period arch.**

*esbatement en ménestrandrie, car moult bien s'y congnoissoit. Il faisoit devant luy voulentiers ses clers chanter et dischanter chansons, rondeaulx et virelais. Il séoit à table environ deux heures, et aussi il veoit bien voulentiers estranges entremets et, iceulx veus, tantost les faisoit envoier par les tables des chevalliers et escuiers."* [2]

And that was just an everyday occurrence! When the Count de Foix held an official banquet, there were dozens of guests. Froissart, once more, wrote that during a Christmas banquet in the Orthez castle, there were four bishops, several counts and numerous lords. The author's style reveals an outmoded world where we get a glimpse of a motley crowd. We can imagine the hubbub of conversations, the sound of the violas, psalterions, pipes and bagpipes. We find it difficult to imagine the infrastructure necessary to host such a crowd.

Fébus owned many fortresses, one of which was Montaner. The castle was built on a hill that dominated the surrounding countryside. It was made up of a fairly large enceinte that was of an almost circular, irregular polygon shape. The thickness of the walls was not far off three metres and reached a height of more than seven metres. The curtain is supported all round by twenty large fairly protruding buttresses. A XVIIIth century engraving shows that the castle had crenels and was equipped with corbel supported machicolations. Each buttress supported a bartizan with arrow slits that covered the foot of the wall. Inside, the parapet wall walk (no longer there) was reached by a straight stairway. The palace has not survived but we can reconstruct it. The court was built around a central building that housed a well. A long, covered gallery served several comfortable single floored lodgings, a large room and the kitchens. There is, in the south, on the attack side, a large 35 metres high square gate keep measuring 13,70 metres along its side. This was used as a residence as well as for defensive purposes as can be seen with the wide bay windows that light up the upper floors. The first floor has a stone arch, the others had wooden floors and were reached by a spiral staircase set in the northeast corner. Each floor had a fireplace. A terse inscription leaves no doubt as to who had them made: *"Febus me fe"* (Fébus made me).

---

2. *"When he left his room half way through the night to take supper in his hall, there were, before him, twelve flaming torches held by twelve servants. These torches were then held in front of his table and brought great light to the hall. This hall was full of knights and equerries, the tables always set for those who desired to take supper. No one spoke to him unless he was invited to do so. Usually he ate an abundance of poultry, especially the thighs and wings. The following day, at dinner (even though it was the most important meal of the day) he ate and drank little. He often took great pleasure in admiring the performances, a subject he knew well. He would not hesitate in making his clerks, be they ten or alone, sing rondos or virelays. He remained at the table for around two hours and during this time, joyfully watched strange performances. Once he had seen them, he straightaway sent them off to the tables of the knights and equerries."*

# The great hall: a public living space

The great hall was the central part of a castle. It was certainly not a new concept as they already existed in nearly all the fortresses built before the XIVth century. Several can be seen in the Bayeux tapestry (XIth century). In Norman Style, they were generally placed on the first floor of big keeps but were sometimes built at its foot. We can take, as an example, the Exchequer room in the Caen castle (XIIth century), or that of the counts palace in Poitiers, built by Henry II Plantagenet (end of XIIth century). These are the direct descendants of the ancient *aulae*, the living quarters in the residences of the first lords. Much attention, however, was now placed on their layout and decor. There was nothing more important than the prince's comfort! In Poitiers, for example, Jean de Berry modernised the northern gable of the ancient building. Three magnificent fireplaces were added and a beautiful glass window inserted, bringing heat and light to the duke sat on his platform. From his pedestal, he looked over his crowd of guests, loyal supporters and those accountable to him. He kept the table open, decided the outcome over disputes between his subjects or intervened in any matters that

The machicolations on the keep at Ponts-de-Cé.

necessitated his decision. The great hall was a multi purpose place that could be adapted according to the needs of the moment. The hall, in normal times, was completely bare, filled when needed with simple furniture such as trestle tables and benches. The taste for pomp and luxury lead to an increasing interest for murals but also, above all, for tapestries, purchased at great expense. The inventory, dated March 11, 1422, of King Charles VI's tapestries, impresses not only by its wealth but also by its quantity. The fabulous *Tenture de l'Apocalypse*, that can still be seen at the castle of Angers, was commissioned by Prince Louis Ist d'Anjou around 1380 and used as decoration at the marriage of Louis II and Yolande d'Aragon in Arles, in 1400.

Let's now place these deserted immense spaces, in the festive context mentioned by Froissart. Imagine the prince, sat slightly higher, feasting on freshly hunted pheasants and wild boar, stoically admiring from his platform, the twirling pirouettes of the acrobats and the precision of the jugglers. He would have also amused himself by listening to the motets and other ballads sung by troubadours or trouvères. They would sing *"doulz viaire gracieux"* by Guillaume de Machaut (1300-1377), which was very fashionable amongst the nobles of the time. A crowd of servants would busy themselves around the monarch and the guests who would enjoy the entertainment and fine food. Even in the middle of the ruins of Mehun, *"the past is merely asleep; for the alert and sensitive mind, all comes to life."* (Jean de La Varende)

*(Continued on page 68)*

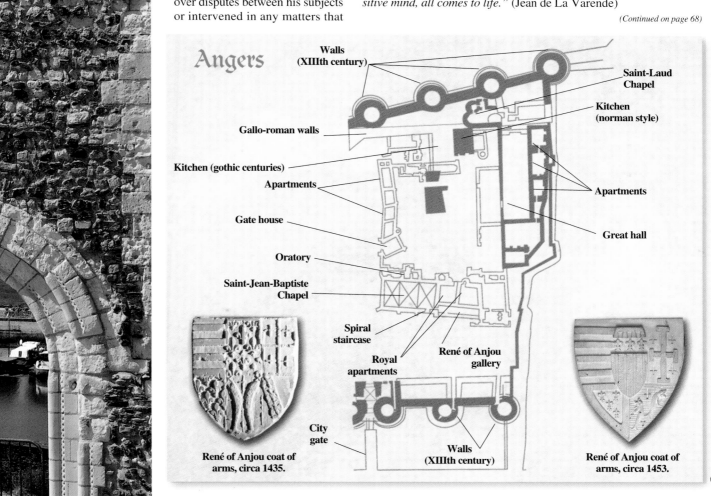

Angers

Walls (XIIIth century)

Saint-Laud Chapel

Kitchen (norman style)

Gallo-roman walls

Kitchen (gothic centuries)

Apartments

Apartments

Gate house

Great hall

Oratory

Saint-Jean-Baptiste Chapel

Spiral staircase

René of Anjou gallery

Royal apartments

René of Anjou coat of arms, circa 1435.

City gate

Walls (XIIIth century)

René of Anjou coat of arms, circa 1453.

61

# Mehun-sur-Yèvre

There was also a fortification at Mehun from the IXth century but the origins of the site are probably far older. The place name, derived from the Celtic dunum, meaning strong place, leaves no doubt about it.

The fortress ended up with the de Courtenay family at the beginning of the XIIIth century, who completely rebuilt the castle in order for it to comply

*(Continued on page 66)*

*Opposite page and the double page 64-65.*
**Castle palace of Mehun-sur-Yèvre. The restoration with the flooded moats is in keeping with the spirit of the miniature taken from the *"Très Riches Heures du Duc de Berry"*. The limited surface area meant that the architect in charge of the construction, had to work vertical miracles.**
*(Reconstruction by Cyrille Castellant, richesheures.com)*

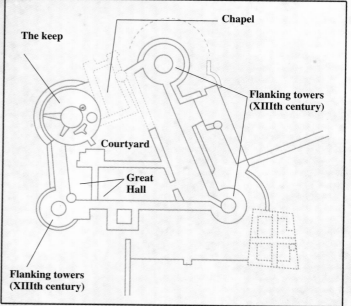

with the standards of Phillip August. A trapezoid is flanked on each corner by a large, jutting out cylinder. The north tower is larger than the others and was the main tower. Mehun fell into the hands of the house of Artois by way of marriage and remained thus until the banishment of Robert III, the famous scarlet giant in Maurice Druon's "*Les Rois Maudits*" (*The Accursed Kings*). Jean II the Good, gave the fortress, along with the Berry to his son Jean as

his prerogative. As was the case with Louis d'Anjou at Saumur, Jean de Berry, from 1370, built an incredible vertical palace on the foundations of a XIIIth century castle. The narrow nature of the site led the architect to use all of his skills to complete a unique jewel of unequalled splendour. King Charles VII died within its walls in 1461. The castle was sadly abandoned in the XVIth century and was methodically destroyed until the XIXth century.

*Above.*
**The ground floor
of the gallery
at the castle of Angers.**

*Opposite.*
**Upper floor
of the gallery, giving
the castle of Angers, one
of medieval
architecture's first
corridors.**

*(Continued from page 61)*

## The private areas: The apartments

If, in essence, the great hall represented the public part of the castle, the apartments, on the other hand, remained for the master of the house and distinguished guests. These parts, therefore, had also to be well lit and heated, comfortable and spacious. Wide mullion windows were set into the thick walls. They were, as has been previously shown, equipped with stone benches where people could rest whilst reading some richly illuminated book of psalms. The beautiful monumental chimneys, sometimes finely crafted (Vincennes), helped to keep up a pleasant and constant atmosphere, even in the middle of winter. Tapestries and wood panelling covered the walls. Furniture became increasingly more refined, caskets, credence tables and chests of all sizes now filled up the various living quarters. Canopy beds also appeared.

Medieval architects, with a few rare and late exceptions (Montaner, Angers), did not use corridors. The different rooms were, therefore, placed horizontally in enfilade. In order to safeguard the prince's privacy or the confidentiality of his work, there was an increase in screening areas between his rooms and the more accessible areas. Each lord also wanted a personal chapel with a clergyman in attendance so that he could lose himself, when needed, in soul saving orisons or take mass. Note finally that gardens became more widespread and sought after as places of pleasure.

Christine de Pisan summed up in a few words this extraordinary way of life when she mentioned the German emperor's visit to France. *"King Charles V accompanied the Roman king to his room of Irish wood, overlooking the gardens and the Sainte-Chapelle, that he had so finely furnished for him."*

Naturally, the numerous servants did not live in such luxury and lived in huge outhouses. They were also housed in the overcrowded garrets where changes in temperature were keenly felt. The enormous kitchens were constantly busy with chefs, spit workers and servants. Their role was to ensure the daily supply of the estate and the house. Whilst all this was going on, the stables were busy with grooms looking after the precious chargers and palfreys. The castle was, therefore, a place that was full of life and where all sorts of professions and talents rubbed shoulders, all with the sole purpose of keeping the lord and his court happy.

## The military "robe"

However, this continual quest for comfort must not hide these stunning castles' main vocation: the protection of the owners and their people against an outside world that did not always harbour the best intentions towards them. Those who suffered from hunger had little esteem for those they deemed responsible for their hardships. The great Jacquerie of 1358 (French peasant rebellion) was a cruel reminder to the noblemen of the Ile-de-France of the reality of the situation.

The English were also on the prowl, even if they did, in general, carefully avoid strongly defended places. They also had the impertinence to lay siege without so much as a warning. More dangerous still, the armed gangs of routiers, dressed in tattered rags, haunted the countryside as they sought sustenance or plunder. In Paris, the King himself was not immune from insurrection. Charles V knew this better than anyone, he had, in his youth, suffered the humiliations imposed upon him by the provost Etienne Marcel.

These military strongholds needed, therefore, in such a climate of insecurity, to impress and dissuade any potential attacker. They were, in consequence, progressively reinforced and had added to them several extremely remarkable technological improvements. The big princely castles built *ex-nihilo* or completely rebuilt, were generally constructed according to geometrically simple plans or structures made popular by Phillip type architecture. The most common shapes could be the triangle (le Clain, in Poitiers), the trapezium (Saumur) or the rectangle (Pierrefonds).

## Looking down on the enemy

Curtain walls and towers began to increase in height. According to Michel Bur, this trend began with the evolution in techniques of attacks with scaling ladders towards the middle of the XIVth century. One needs to be careful with this conclusion, other factors would have certainly led architects to adapt to the fighting methods of the day. Perhaps we should first take into account the massive use of the crossbow in siege warfare and its increasing improvement (metal bow, ballista). Known in antiquity but almost completely disappeared during the upper middle ages, we come across it in the narrative of the Vikings' siege of Paris (885-886) and a few XIth century texts ("*Carmen de Hastinae proelio*" - Song of the Battle of Hastings-, "*Vita Willelmi*" - Life of William the Conqueror -, "*Alexiade*"). The council of Latran in 1139 banned its use in the wars between Christians and threatened anyone who persisted in using it with excommunication. It was, in any case, a crossbow bolt that ended Richard the Lion Heart's life in 1199. Existing inventories show the weapon's omnipresence in the armouries of the garrisons during the last 60 years of the XIIIth century and the first thirty years of the XIVth century. The bow seemingly remained the weapon of choice. The years between 1230 and 1340 were a relatively peaceful period in the kingdom and the crossbows remained

*(Continued on page 72)*

*Above.* **The tower of Baris at Jerusalem. The tower walls are set with arrow slit-canonniers, the summit had a crenellated parapet. Speculum humanae salvationis, 1462.**
*(Bibl. mun. de Lyon, Ms 245 f° 126.*
*Photograph Bibliothèque municipale de Lyon, Didier Nicole.)* 69

# Artistic machicolations

**T**HE WIDE SCALE
*use of machicolations in the new
buildings or renovations of the XIVth
and XVth centuries, gave them
a characteristic aspect.*

Stonecutters quickly monopolized this new market to show off their talent and imagination. In Brittany, from very early on, they used reversed half pyramids, like at Suscinio or Largöet-en-Elven (Morbihan). Near the Rhône valley and in the Languedoc, they preferred the long, slender, multiple stepped corbels. This is notably the case at the Fortress of Saint-André at Villeneuve-lès-Avignon (Gard).

Different types cheerfully crossed the borders however. The fine quality machicolations on the tower of Vidame in Tiffauges (Vendée), built in the XVIth century, are reminiscent of those at Tarascon (Bouches-du-Rhône). Brittany inspired machicolations can be seen at the top of the Big Tower of Bonaguil (Lot-et-Garonne). At Mehun-sur-Yèvre, the cornices are sculpted and adorned with triple lobed motifs.

This last touch of architectural style can be seen on many buildings, but first prize for aesthetics must go to the magnificent small tower of Pannessac in Puy-en-Velay, that is surprising in the subtlety of its decoration.

**5**

**6**

**7**

1. Machicolations with triple lobed motifs, castle of Chinon.

2. Briton machicolations (reversed pyramids), with triple lobed motifs. Castle of Clisson.

3. The lantern tower at La Rochelle (XIVth – XVth centuries).

4. Fort Saint-André, Villeneuve-les-Avignon. *(Photo Yann Kervran)*

5. Corbelled machicolations. Château de la Ferté-Milon.

6. Montsoreau.

7. The chain tower at La Rochelle.

8. Machicolations on the La Rochelle town hall.

**8**

**Bench window. Castle of Blandy-les-Tours.**
*(Photo Cyrille Castellant)*

*(Continued from page 69)*

where they were on the racks. This was not comparable, therefore, with the constant insecurity that characterised the Hundred Years War. Those who were building could not, from now on, ignore the systematic use of the crossbow and had to take into consideration its potential in their building parameters. When shot upwards, the crossbow bolt undeniably lost its firepower and soon adopted a parabolic trajectory. The heavy weight of the weapon (10-12 kilos) also meant that it was exhausting to use and was, in consequence, difficult to aim with precision. Inversely, when fired from the wall walk, its power and precision increased. This observation went hand in hand with the multiplication of stirrup arrow slits and, above all, the English influence of arrow slits with a crosspiece (cruciform arrow slits) that made it easier to handle and fire crossbows. This was notably the case in Villandraut or Roquetaillade (Gironde), built in the first years of the XIVth century, or in the Popes' Palace in Avignon. Finally, we note the progressive disappearance of arrow slits at the base of towers and curtain walls. They were sometimes replaced by big barred windows with no defensive vocation, closed by a thick, wooden interior shutter. Once more, the cursed weapon's efficiency and feared accuracy probably had something to do with it. A small hole could easily be hit by an elite crossbowman from quite low down and the defender was not safe from a well-aimed bolt. Arrow slits were now, therefore, only set in the high parts of a building.

It also seems necessary to mention the development of increasingly sophisticated and higher siege weaponry. Mobile siege towers became higher as carpenters' skills increased. During the siege of

Breteuil in 1356, for example, Jean II the Good had an enormous mobile siege tower made (quickly destroyed, I may add) so that he could reach the walls of the rebel citadel, which surprised chroniclers by its exceptional size. One must not neglect, above all, the arrival of the first firearms around 1350. In the beginning they did not have the destructive capacities of popular belief. Froissart was more impressed with the noise that came from these thunderous, smoking weapons, than with the damage they caused. *"Quant celle bombarde descliquoit, on l'ooit par jour bien. V lieus loing, et par nuit. X"*[3]. For a long time yet, crossbows and other catapults would play a role alongside bombardes and canons. The latter, however, evolved considerably in the first part of the XVth century. Using them became easier from now on and their range, power and precision progressively increased, which did not go unnoticed by the people of the time. Monstrelet witnessed the destructive power of the bombardes during the siege of Meaux by Henry of Lancaster in 1422. *"Il gaigna une petite ysle assez près du marchié, en laquelle il fit asseoir plusieurs grosses bombardes, qui moult terriblement craventèrent les maison dudit marchié et aussi les murailles d'icellui"*[4]. In order to combat flat trajectory and parabolic shots, the architects respectively thickened the walls and made them higher.

The basic symbol that the castle represented in feudal society should also be remembered. The power base in a hostile environment, it consequently had to impress, with its high towers and curtain walls, the people and their seditious ways but also the marauding enemy. It was a stone symbol of the power of its owner.

---

3. *"When this bombarde was fired, it was heard, during daylight over five leagues away, and by night, ten."*
4. *"He reached a small island bear the fortress and installed several large bombardes that horribly tore apart the houses and walls of the said place."*

# The Louvre of Charles V

*HRISTINE DE PISAN summed up so well the comforts that great princely fortresses were supposed to provide at the end of the XIVth century.*

When she mentioned the visit of the Germanic Emperor, Charles IV, to the symbolic castle of the French monarchy. She also talks of the undeniable intention to dazzle the prestigious guest.

*"Lendemain volt aller le Roy disner au Louvre; et à la pointe du pallaiz fu porté l'Empereur: là estoit le bel batel du Roy, qui estoit fait et ordonné comme une belle maison; là entrèrent et prisa moult ce beau batel l'Empereur. Au Louvre arriverent. Le Roy monstra à l'Empereur les beauls murs et maçonnages qu'il avoit fait au Louvre édifier; l'Empereur, son filz et ses barons moult bien y logia, et partout estoit le lieu moult richement paré; en sale disna le Roy, les barons avec lui, et l'empereur en sa chambre."*[1]

Apart from the description of the pomp, the text shows some interesting details on the lines of communication established by Charles V between his different palaces situated at the gates of his capital. He could, therefore, leave the city in order to reach the Louvre, without passing along the streets of Paris. The wise King, did not want, at any cost, to find himself the captive of an unpredictable people as had been the case at the time of Etienne Marcel.

---

1. *" The following day, the King wanted to dine at the Louvre; the Emperor was taken to the tip of the Louvre where a beautiful boat of the King awaited. It was arranged like a beautiful house, so well painted on the outside and decorated inside. They boarded it and the Emperor was much taken by the beautiful boat. They arrived at the Louvre. The King showed him the wonderful walls and carvings that he had ordered to made. The Emperor was comfortably installed along with his son and his barons, and everywhere the place was richly decorated. The King dined in his room along with his barons and the Emperor in dined in his chamber."*

1 219. Charles V receives the German emperor Charles IV. Court life inside a castle palace was of an unheard of luxury. The picture shown goes well with the description given by Christine de Pisan. Whilst the king eats with his guest and a host of prelates, the king of England attacks a fortress. Grandes Chroniques de France, circa 1375 *(Paris, Bibl. nat. de France Ms. Fr. 2813 f° 473 v°)*

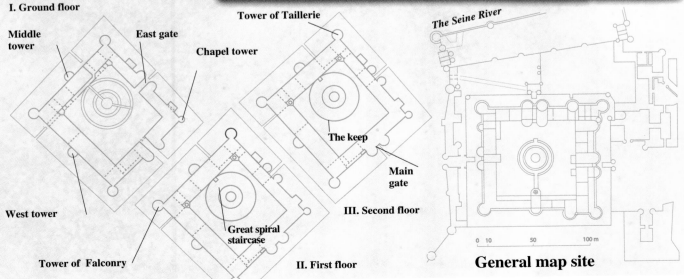

**I. Ground floor**

Middle tower

East gate

West tower

Tower of Falconry

Tower of Taillerie

Chapel tower

The keep

Main gate

Great spiral staircase

**III. Second floor**

**II. First floor**

*The Seine River*

0  10       50       100 m

**General map site**

# Andlau and Poitiers

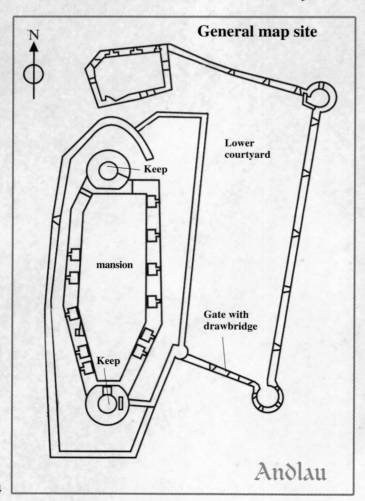

**General map site**

N

Lower
courtyard

Keep

mansion

Gate with
drawbridge

Keep

Andlau

*Above and following page.*
**The duke's palace at Poitiers, the Maubergeon tower and the southern gable of the great hall.**

74

*Opposite and following page.*
The Maubergeon tower dates from the XIIth century, but it was completely overhauled for the Duc Jean of Berry, so that it conformed to XIVth century tastes. There are many sculptures and statues.

*Pages 78 and 79.*
The great hall was built for Henri II Plantagenet, but underwent modifications by Jean of Berry. The southern gable had a huge window placed in it, flooding the interior with natural light. Today it is the *"salle des pas perdus"* (hall of lost footsteps) at the courthouse.

*Pages 80-81.*
The three huge fireplaces heated the duke's back as he sat on the platform. They mainly bear the coat of arms of France and Jean of Berry.

## Defending from the high spots

The standard fortress of the years between 1350 and 1450 therefore greatly increased in height. Towers no longer clearly commanded the curtain walls as they had in the past. In certain new and compact castles, all vantage points were even equalised, thus making a huge platform upon which defenders could move freely and if need be, set up weaponry. In this highly specific monoblock family is the castle at Tarascon (Bouches-du-Rhône), destined more as a residence, or the famous Bastille (a huge barbican) essentially for military use, no longer visible today which disap-

*Above.* **The English attacking the fortress of Brest (1386). The castle shown is directly derived from that of the Bastille. The towers and curtain walls are of the same height, the tops have a wall walk with continuous machicolations. The counter balance beam drawbridge is half down. Jean Froissart's Chronicles, end of the XVth century.**
*(Paris, Bibl. nat. de France Ms. Fr. 2645 f° 116 v°)*

*Opposite.*
**A scene from the Punic wars: the siege of Capoue by the Carthagian armies (212-211 B.C.) The attack is shown in a XIVth century style. The crossbow is omnipresent and the attackers launch their assault on the ramparts using long ladders. History of Rome, Tite-Live.**
*(Bibl. nat. de France Ms. Fr. 32 f° 84)*

*Opposite page.*
**One of the emblazoned entrances at the castle of Avignon.**
*(Photo Yann Kervrant)*

Palais
des
Papes

*Above.* **Castle of Berzy-le-Sec.**

*Opposite.*
**The Curemonte tower and its ring of machicolations.**

*Following page, from top to bottom.*
**Fort Saint-André at Villeneuve-les-Avignon.**

**Small bretèche. Fort Saint-André at Villeneuve-les-Avignon.**
*(Photos Yann Kervran)*

peared during the first days of the French Revolution. The fortress of Brest (Finistère) also appears in similar form in one of Froissart's Chronicles manuscripts.

Without returning to the outmoded concept of passive defence, the architects imposed that of defence from the high spots. The arrow slits set high up were joined by traditional merlons and crenels but also, and above all, by a clever system that really caught on from 1350 onwards, machicolations supported by corbels.

The machicolations were openings on top of towers and curtain walls, allowing for vertical fire on the enemy. In the XIVth century, they were not a real innovation. It seems certain that they were in use in the Holy Land in the first third of the XIIth century (Sahyoun in what is today, Syria). They were, however, at that time, large arches curved over buttresses. This system was notably used at Niort (Deux-Sevres), around 1180 and at Château-Gaillard (Eure) built between 1196 and 1197. They were also found at Lucheux (Somme) towards the end of the XIIth century or

*(Continued on page 90)*

# Tarascon

**Tarascon had, without doubt, been a fortified site since far-off times. Its key position on the left bank of the river Rhône, opposite Beaucaire, the ancient Ugernum, meant that it very quickly became a strategic site.**

The *"Chanson de la Croisade Albigoise"*, perfectly illustrates this importance in the words that it attributes to Raymond VI de Toulouse. As a recommendation to his son, Raymondet (literally *"The little Raymond"*, the future Raymond VII), who wished to take Beaucaire, he supposedly said: *"Look after those of Tarascon in the same way. Be good, generous, make them adore you as you cannot, without them, take Beaucaire. Their armed boatmen must seal all access to the rock on which the ramparts are made. Without water, Beaucaire will fall."*

The castle underwent a first, complete restoration in 1292, upon the orders of Charles II d'Anjou. The castle was damaged between 1367 and 1382 and was once more completely rebuilt from 1400, by the Anjou-Provence dynasty, in theory if not in fact, the rulers of Naples. The famous Good King René, enlightened patron, art lover and sometimes poet (*"Le Livre du Cuer d'Amours espris"*, around 1457), made it of his favourite residences. Tarascon was, at that time, a redoubtable border fortress, as well as a comfortable residence, between the Kingdom of France and the county of Provence. It lost its strategic importance on the death of Count Charles III (1481), who had, beforehand, designated King Louis XI as the heir of all that he owned.

Tarascon was the scene of fighting one last time in 1652, during the series of civil wars known as the Fronde. It became a state prison in the XVIIIth century and remained so until 1926.

*Opposite.*
**King René by David d'Angers in Angers.**

*At the top and opposite, on the right.*
**The castle of Tarascon, built by the Anjou-Provence.**
**This is an example of the monoblock family of fortresses.**
**The towers and curtains are the same height, as with the Bastille in Paris, and, to a lesser extent, La Ferté-Milon. The moats could be flooded buy using the water from the Rhône.**
*(Photos Yann Kervran)*

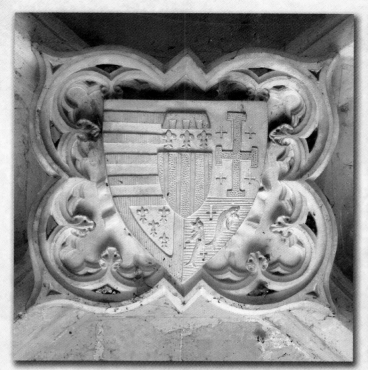

*Above, from right to left.*
**The coat of arms of René d'Anjou evolved throughout the course of his life, depending on his good fortune or his returns to glory. (1453 on the left and 1435 on the right). Emblazoned keystones at the castle of Angers.**

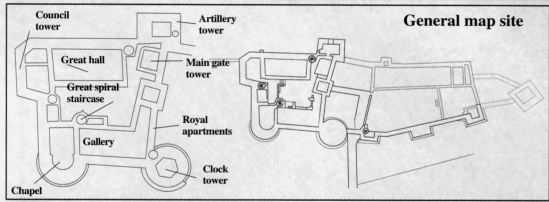

**General map site**

Council tower

Great hall

Great spiral staircase

Gallery

Chapel

Artillery tower

Main gate tower

Royal apartments

Clock tower

The gate house (*châtelet*) at Berzy-le-Sec.

Siege of Bayonne (1451). The winch crossbow meant that the enemy could be fired at with a rare accuracy. The population has taken refuge behind the walls and pulled up the drawbridge.
**Vigiles of Charles VII by Martial d'Auvergne, 1484.**
*(Paris, Bibl. nat. de France Ms. Fr. 5054 f°219)*

Siege of Bellême by the duc d'Alençon (1449). A large bombarde and its stone projectiles are prepared in order to attack the high walls with their arrow slits and canonniers.
**Vigiles of Charles VII by Martial d'Auvergne, 1484.**
*(Paris, Bibl. nat. de France Ms. Fr. 5054 f° 188 v°)*

*Above.*
**The Philippe the Fair tower at Villeneuve-les-Avignon. Built circa 1300, The machicolations were added several decades later.**
*(Photo Yann Kervran)*

*Opposite, on the right.* **Siege of Derval (Loire-Atlantique) in 1373. Very slender and perfectly within the spirit of the XIVth and XVth centuries, the fortress had a large barbican and was surrounded by wide moats. The towers and the curtains had wooden hoardings and not machicolations. The counter balance beam drawbridges are lowered. Compilation of Breton chronicles and history by Pierre le Baud, circa 1480.** *(Paris, Bibl. nat. de France Ms. Fr. 8266 f° 281)*

*Following page.*
**The drawbridge at the castle of Suscinio in the Morbihan.**

*(Continued from page 84)*

at the beginning of the next, and also at Farcheville (Essone) at the beginning of the XIVth century. They were also used from time to time on religious buildings of varying importance, the cathedral d'Agde (Hérault), the Sainte-Catherine tower in Albi (Tarn), part of the same town's old Bishop's residence. They can also be seen on a few urban buildings such as the Porte d'Ardon, in Laon (Aisne) in the beginning of the XIIth century, or the Porte de Sens in Villeneuve-sur-Yonne (Yonne). The surprising *"Machicolations building"* in Le Puy (Haute-Loire), also dating from the XIIth century, is a rare example of alternating between arched machicolations over buttresses and those on corbels. The first of its kind.

The change seems to have come from the Holy Land, when the Mameluk sultan Baibars conquered the legendary castle, the Krak des Chevaliers after hard fighting in 1271. The Syrian fortress had suffered badly in the siege and large-scale reconstruction was necessary for its restoration. The Arab engineers equipped the wall walk with numerous, closely spaced bretèches that almost acted as machicolations. The idea, slightly modified to an uninterrupted succession of stone corbels, spread as far as the west. It seems that from the beginning of the XIVth century, the solution came to the architect responsible for the donjon at Bourdeilles (Dordogne). This very quickly spread throughout the kingdom and from now on there was hardly a new construction that did not have a crown of machicolations on the summit. The splendid Tours de Merle or of Curemonte (Cor-

90

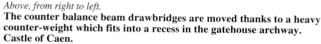

*Above, from right to left.*
**The counter balance beam drawbridges are moved thanks to a heavy counter-weight which fits into a recess in the gatehouse archway. Castle of Caen.**

**The gatehouse (châtelet) at the entrance to the castle of Tarascon.**
*(Photo Yann Kervran)*

*Opposite.* **The counter-weight of a counter balance beam drawbridge. Castle of Vincennes.** *(Photo Cyrille Castellant)*

*Following page, from top to bottom.* **The fortress of Caen. The XIIIth century gatehouse was modified in the XIVth century in order to add a counter balance beam drawbridge and a fine row of machicolations.**

**The gate at the castle of Clisson with cart and foot drawbridges.**

rèze), the palaces of Ferté-Milon, Pierrefonds, Mehun-sur-Yèvre, the old Norman Style keeps of Moncontour (Vienne), Pouzages (Vendée), Château-Chervix (Haute-Vienne), Chambois (Orne) and many others were similarly equipped. The hoardings, that the machicolations progressively replaced did not, however, disappear totally from the older buildings. The *"Armorial de Revel"* (XVth century), clearly shows the castle of la Haye-Bénisson (Loire) equipped with wooden superstructures. The oldest hoardings that have survived to modern times, with the exception of the castle of Laval (XIIIth century), date precisely from the XVth and XVIth centuries: La Motte-Feuilly (Indre) or Culan (Cher). There are, jutting out very high up on the corners, small turrets that were defensive positions where one or two defenders could take up positions. The flanks of the curtain walls were thus better covered.

## The counter balance beam drawbridge

The gate was the traditional weak point of all fortresses. Philip August's architects resolved this age old problem by invariably making the point of access between two flanking drum towers equipped with a portcullis, murder holes, vantails and a mobile bridge that could span the ditch. The

*(Continued on page 96)*

# Adapting the arrow slits

HE progressive use of portable firearms meant that masons had to modernize the arrow slits, starting at the beginning of the first third of the XVth century.

It was impossible to use such weapons through the old arrow slits from Phillip August's time and their derivatives. A round hole was therefore pierced in the wall, at the centre of the vertical slit. The sniper could then aim his weapon in any direction. Good examples of arrow slit cannon ports can be still be seen at the castles of Dourdan, Caen, Falaise… and on many other French medieval buildings. When small calibre weapons became more widespread, the architects designed apertures of different shapes, horizontal or vertical, known as canonniers

**Canonnier at the castle of Caen.**

**Canonniers at the castle of Caen.**

**Castle of Dourdan. A XIIIth century arrow slit transformed into an arrow-slit-canonnier in the XVth century by making a circular aperture in its centre.**

**Arrow slit with a single aperture, modified for the use of firearms. Castle of Falaise.**

*Above.*
**Small canonnier with aiming cross-piece, a XVth century addition to the old walls of the castle of Péronne.**

*Opposite from left to right.*
**Modified arrow slit to aid the use of fire-arms. Castle of Tancarville.**

**Arrow slit-canonnier at the castle of Gacé.**

94

The gate house
at Montreuil-Bellay,
with a single cart drawbridge.

*Above and following page.* **Castle of Vitré.**

*Opposite, on the right.* **The French take the town and castle of Duras (Lot-et-Garonne) in 1377. The man in the foreground re-loads a powerful winch crossbow. His companions assault the high walls with machicolations thanks to long ladders. Jean Froissart's Chronicles, end of the XVth century.** *(Paris, Bibl. nat. de France Ms. Fr. 2644 f° 9)*

**Page 98. A foot drawbridge defended by a small *bretèche*. Castle of Clisson.**

*(continued from page 92)*

latter required the use of chains, attached to the footway of the bridge as well as small holes set into the walls to allow the chains to pass through and the fixation of winches that were operated by several people positioned on the first floor.

A new system appeared in the middle of the XIVth century that simplified the operating of the bridge. This was the drawbridge using a counter balance beam which was surprisingly easy in design, although someone had to think of it first. When the bridge was lowered, an enormous counterweight fitted into its emplacement in the vault of the specially made building. There were two large parallel beams that passed through the walls, connected at the outer ends to the footway. If the gateway needed to be tightly sealed, all it took was to pull the counterweight towards oneself. The drawbridge would then rise and the outer beams would fall back into the vertical recesses in the face of the wall. Generally in pairs, the latter can be easily made out on the facades of many fortresses: Blain (Loire-Atlantique), Lavardin, Berzy (Aisne), Pirou (Manche), Montreuil-Bellay (Maine-et-Loire), La Roche-Goyon (Côtes-d'Armor), Caen…

The cart bridge was often accompanied by a footbridge. In these cases there are often three or even four recesses. This can be seen at Montmuran and Combourg (Ille-et-Vilaine), Tarascon, Largöet-en-Elven, Tonquédec (Côtes-d'Armor), Clisson…

The growth in counter balance beam drawbridges was accompanied by an increase in the attention that was paid to the construction of ditches. Often paved, they were, from now on, more often filled with water when

*Opposite.*
**The siege of Caen by the French (1450).**
**The king personally takes charge of operations.**
**The fortress drawbridge is preceded by a simple**
**wooden barbican, a reminder of the persistent**
**and late use of his material in the art of fortifications.**
**Vigiles of Charles VII by Martial d'Auvergne, 1484.**
*(Paris, Bibl. nat. de France Ms. Fr. 5054 f°199)*

## Barbicans, ravelins
## and boulevards

These three words are in fact quite synonyms. Always with a view to reinforcing the defensive system of the gate, the period between 1350 and 1450 saw an increase in advanced stone defence works, commonly known as barbicans. The oldest known example in France dates from the XIIIth century and can be found at Carcassonne (Aude).

With the end of the XIVth century and the dawn of the XVth century, countless ravelins now stood in the way of potential attackers. Two magnificent examples can be seen at Caen (Calvados). Other fine examples are still visible at Sillé-le-Guillaume (Sarthe), Brest and Présilly (Jura).

*(Continued on page 102)*

*Below.*
**The *Porte des Champs* at the castle of Caen and its barbican.**

# Machicolations. Beware of fakes!

 **ACHICOLATIONS at the top of a castle are not always the absolute proof of an addition or a creation dating from the XIVth-XVth centuries.**

The renovators of the XIXth century often resorted to this process when they were, according to their own aesthetic criteria, led to renovate the buildings of their predecessors. In this way, the ring of corbels added to the Archives tower at Vernon (Eure) is not contemporary to the building.

*Opposite, left.*
**Archives tower at Vernon.**

*Below and following page.*
**The *Porte des Champs* at the castle of Caen and its barbican.**

*Above and opposite.*
**The octagonal keep at Largoët-en-Elven.**
*(Photos Cyrille Castellant)*

*Following page.*
**The keep at Oudon is very similar to that at Largoët.**
**The men who had them built were brothers.**

*Page 104-105.*
**The quadrangular keep in Polignac is built**
**on the top of a dizzy dyke.**

*(Continued from page 99)*

Do not believe for a minute that wood had totally disappeared from this type of construction. The illustration of la Haye-Bénisson, found in the *"l'Armorial de Revel"*, which we have already mentioned with its hoardings, shows a succession of palissades built in front of the fortress and designed to slow down an enemy's advance. These defence works can be seen in many other illuminations. The strength of the materials used depended on… the strength of the owner's purse!

## The residential keep makes its come back

The men in charge of Philip Auguste's projects had designed fortresses where the main tower, always of a circular shape, was only relatively important. In Dourdan (Essone), the most accomplished example of early XIIIth century architecture, the large tower was moved to the edge of the enceinte, on the attack side. It no longer had any residential function. At La Fère-en-Tardenois (Aisne), built by Count Robert II de Dreux after 1206, or Boulogne-sur-Mer (Pas-de-Calais), built by Philipp Hurepel before 1231, the tower had quite simply disappeared.

In the first decades of the Hundred Years War, this standard plan lost ground and the residential keep came back with a vengeance. This trend manifested itself mostly with noblemen of lesser importance but also, occasionally, with those of a higher standing. The

*(Continued on page 108)*

*Opposite and following page.*
**The residential Saint-Nicolas tower at La Rochelle (second half of the XIVth century).**

*below, on the right.*
**The Solidor tower, at Saint-Malo.**
*(Photo Cyrille Castellant)*

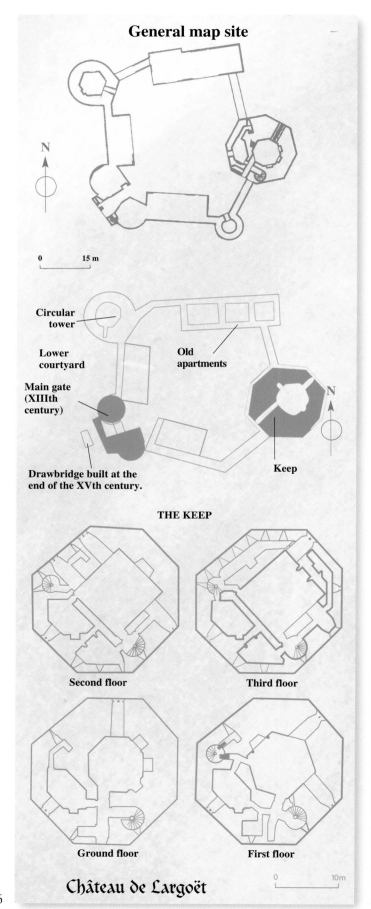

# General map site

0          15 m

N

**Circular tower**

**Lower courtyard**

**Old apartments**

**Main gate (XIIIth century)**

N

**Drawbridge built at the end of the XVth century.**

**Keep**

### THE KEEP

**Second floor**

**Third floor**

**Ground floor**

**First floor**

*Château de Largoët*

0          10m

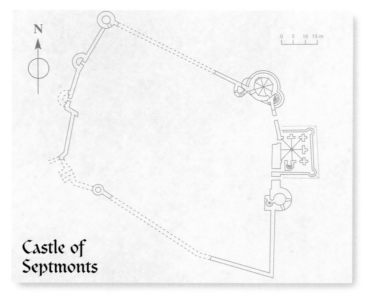

## Castle of Septmonts

*(continued from page 102)*

influence of Vincennes can be seen here, and, by emulation, Dijon. The circular shape that made the occupation of the interior difficult, was generally abandoned. There are some noteworthy exceptions, such as the prestigious Saint-Nicolas tower at La Rochelle or the fabulous donjon at Septmonts. We therefore come back to the traditional quadrangular shape at Polignac (Haute-Loire), Vez, Chateâugay (Puy-de-Dome), Moricq (Vendée), Bassoue (Gers), Mauvezin. The keep could also be square or rectangular, flanked by large cylinders on the corners, as with the castles of Val and Anjony (Cantal) or Sarzay. Other, more original shapes, mostly polygonal, can be seen at Oudon or Tancarville. These keeps, of a relatively archaic design, were inspired more by the XIth and XIIth century fortresses than by Phillip August's example.

Largöet-en-Elven incarnates the archetype of these new rural castles. It consists of a confined polygonal enceinte. The small area that it covers meant that fewer defenders would be needed to guard it. It is surrounded by deep, wide moats, which were flooded thanks to the proximity of the small river Arz. The moats were crossed using two counter balance beam drawbridges (one for carts the other for pedestrians) that were defended by a flat-faced gatehouse crowned with machicolations. The splendid coat of arms of the Lords de Rieux, carved into the stone between the two vertical recesses for the foot drawbridge beams, is a reminder of the power once held by the Lords of the castle. The gatehouse is made up of two distinct parts, twin towers with arrow slits in the purest architectural tradition of the XIIIth century, and a building that was added at the end of the XVth century.

The courtyard, in bygone times, was occupied by several residential buildings. At the western side, a large, slightly oblong shaped tower, cut the curtain. Its canonniers and its general appearance date it more to the end of the XVth century. It is also reminiscent in many ways of other contemporary buildings such as the Raoul towers or Surienne of Fougères. However, the most fabulous part of the site is without doubt the enormous octagonal donjon, that from its height of 44 metres, dominates the entire place. It measures, at its widest part, nearly 24 metres and the walls reach 7 metres at the base. The donjon has its own moat and counter balance beam drawbridge. Inside, there are six rooms. A spiral staircase set into the southern wall and starting at the ground floor, provides access to all the upper floors. From the first floor, a second, smaller staircase, in the north this time, makes access easier. Each floor had wooden floorboards, was heated and had latrines. The upper rooms had a surface area of 100 square metres and included latrines. The top of the donjon had a walkway that was equipped with briton machicolations. There are even finely sculpted triple lobed motifs between each reverse pyramid corbel. This magnificent lord's residence was built by Jean II de Malestroit around 1375. It combines all of the period's residential imperatives without losing out on the military side.

Generally, high towers of this type allowed their owners to conspicuously show their own power, as they saw it, reminding the local peasants who held the power over the surrounding land. In these residences, designed for their comfort, often well lit and heated, they reproduced the court life of the mighty of the world and took efficient precautions against attack by small gangs of human predators on the look out for plunder.

It is, therefore, difficult to paint a standard picture of a castle during the Hundred Years War, as there is so much diversity. Many different things have to be taken into account and each fortress has its own particularities. There seem to be two main points that dominate policy in the making of castles during this troubled period: the constant quest for comfort allied with the unshakeable desire to insure ones safety. André Chatelain sums up perfectly the criteria popular of the period when he underlines the " rebalancing the habitability of castles in relation to their defensive qualities, the faithfulness to the preferably geometrical plans of the previous century and the renewed interest in the keeps, which were most often square and habitable."

**The Roman army riding in great pomp… XVth century…**
**In the foreground, a river laps against the foot of a fortress.**
**The walls have different types of canonniers.**
**An impressive crenellated parapet protects the wall walk.**
**Tite-Live, History of Rome, mid XVth century.**
*(Paris, Bibl. nat. de France Ms. Fr. 33 f° 233 v°)*

# The castles of Louis d'Orléans

## La Ferté-Milon

*The younger brother of Charles VI, Louis d'Orléans took advantage of his brother's mental illness to get his hands on the royal treasure.*

Dipping into the monarchy's coffers whenever it pleased him, he was able to satisfy his inordinate taste for luxury, the lavish court life and the sometimes strange festivities. He also began a gigantic programme of castle construction on the Valois lands. He had Pierrefonds completely rebuilt from 1396, on the foundations of a pre-existing modest castle. There were recesses in the towers in which were placed statues of the Nine Waliant Knights, mythical or real warriors from ancient history (Cesar, Charlemagne, Arthur, Alexandre…). His second construction started in 1398 at La Ferté-Milon. The monumental facade rose slowly, this time under the patronage of the Nine Worthy Women, heroines from antiquity or women saints of the Christian faith. At the same time, Orléans finished the work begun by Enguerrand VII at Coucy. His violent death in 1407, brought

*(continued on page 114)*

Only the façade of La Ferté-Milon was finished. Louis d'Orléans'death, in 1407, put a definitive end to the construction. The monumental power of the edifice hits one straight away.
The cyclopean door, inserted between the two almond shaped towers reinforces this impression.

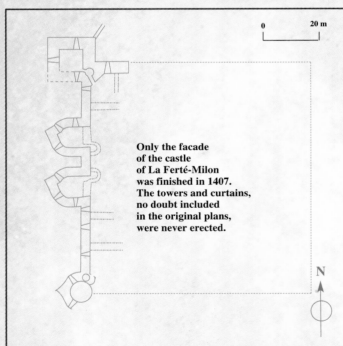

Only the facade
of the castle
of La Ferté-Milon
was finished in 1407.
The towers and curtains,
no doubt included
in the original plans,
were never erected.

*Previous double page.*
**The crowning of the Virgin is shown above the huge door.**

*Opposite.*
**Recesses ringed with a remarkable frieze have been incorporated
into the towers. They contain a statue of the Nine Worthy Women.**

*(Continued from the page 110)*

all this work to a definitive halt. La Ferté-Milon notably was left as
it was and to this day, remains a crystallised reminder of the delusions of grandeur that gripped France's noblemen at the turn of the
XIVth and XVth centuries.

# Pierrefonds

*Opposite.*
**The recesses in the towers contain statues of the Nine Valiant Knights.
The theme is in relation with that
of the Nine Worthy Women at La Ferté-Milon.**

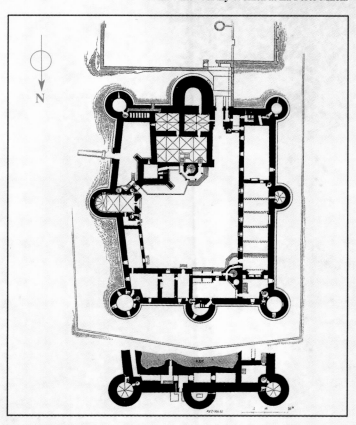

*Opposite and following pages.*
**Entirely rebuilt by Louis d'Orléans before 1407, Pierrefonds underwent a full restoration by Eugène Viollet le Duc in the XIXth century. The castle has become, in collective imagination, the symbol of a Middle Ages ideal.**

# Laissez parler la poudre !

*Let the powder roar!*

Messire Jaques sera tenu de laisser au dit chastel toutes les pouldres, arbalestres et trait sans rien gaster ne despécier, réservés neuf veuglaires et deux cacques de pouldres.[1]

Enguerrand de Monstrelet

HE TURNING POINT in the art of war, came with the first firearms during the Hundred Years War. The strange black powder invented in China for festive use, towards the beginning of the Christian era, soon found a more murderous use in the West.

Gunpowder filled tubes, culverins and bombardes, progressively left the bow, crossbow, ballista and perrier onto the shelves of history. Battles and sieges were now accompanied by the sound of thunder.

## The first use of the "black powder"

Four measures of saltpetre, three of sulphur and three wood charcoal. Mix the different ingredients and you have an explosive cocktail. Just how did this apparently inoffensive Chinese recipe, reach the West? Nobody knows. One can, however, wager that the opening of trade routes with the Far East and the more or less peaceful, but regular, trading with the Arab world has something to do with it. The engineers soon realised the military potential that they could gain from the recipe and learnt how to harness the energy produced by the explosion. Thanks to the powder, they could launch various heavy projectiles over considerable distances. It is, however, impossible to say with certitude when this new weapon was first used in battle. The word bombarde (from the Latin *bombus*, meaning booming sound), or cannon (from the Italian *cannone*, itself augmentative of *canna*, meaning tube), only appeared in the years 1320-1330, thanks to the quills of meticulous and conscientious people who saw them. Most of the chroniclers use vague and ambiguous words, talking of artillery or engines, indifferently grouping together under these generic terms, powder weapons, *pierriers* and other *mangonels*. Unmistakably, it was, in fact, the middle of the XIVth century that saw the frequent use of firearms, the process gaining speed from 1400.

## Bombardes and cannons.

Using the first large calibre weapons was a lot like playing Russian roulette, you were either lucky or not. The men serving the weapon had a much higher chance of blowing up along with it rather than seeing the curtain walls come down at the first shot. The tubes were generally quite short and made in the same way as a barrel. Long staves, slightly curved metallic strips (made depending on the period of copper, iron, bronze, steel or smelt), were soldered together then reinforced by concentric circular pieces made from the same metal. The body of the weapon was not, therefore, made from one solid piece and its robustness was consequently very relative.

In times of siege, the cannon was firstly sited, that is to say it was placed in a large wooden case fixed to the ground by stakes driven deep into the ground. The cannon was then pointed in the direction of its target before being firmly tied down. The crew loaded the cannon via the muzzle (several fruitless attempts to load it via the breech were made). The powder was pushed down with hay or straw, the cannonball was then inserted (initially made of stone and later of iron) in the bore. A member of the crew would then take a red hot poker and place it on the opening that would allow the

The siege of Jerusalem by the Romans in 70 A.D. The attackers have set up a large cannon in order to bombard the city. This type of weapon appeared in the first half of the XIVth century, becoming widespread between 1350 and 1400. Jewish War by Flavius Josèphe, 3rd quarter XVth century.
*(Paris, Bibl. nat. de France Ms. Fr. 249 f° 237)*

## The siege

ORK, your thoughts, and therein see a siege Behold the ordnance on their carriages,

With fatal mouths gaping on girded Harfleur. and the nimble gunner With linstock now the devilish cannon touches, And down goes all before them.

*William Shakespeare, Henry V, Act III, Chorus.*

1. *"My Lord Jacques will be obliged to leave all powder, crossbows and projectiles in the said castle without spoiling anything, with the exception of nine artillery pieces (veuglaires) and two barrels of powder."*

# The first attacks

 **HE plain-song is most just: for humours do abound: Knocks go and come; God's vassals drop and die;**

And sword and shield, In bloody field, Doth win immortal fame… To the mines! tell you the duke, it is not so good to come to the mines; for, look you, the mines is not according to the disciplines of the war: the concavities of it is not sufficient; for, look you, the adversary, you may discuss unto the duke, look you, is digt himself four yard under the countermines: by Cheshu, I think a will plough up all, if there is not better directions."
*William Shakespeare, Henry V, Act III, Scene II.*

*At the top on the left.* **Artillery became mobile, carried on chariots. This meant that large and small weapons could be moved from one siege to another in optimal conditions. Vigiles of Charles VII by Martial d'Auvergne, 1484.**
*(Paris, Bibl. nat. de France Ms. Fr. 5054 f° 101)*

*At the top on the right.* **Flavius Josephus goes to Vespasian. The artillery is made up of heavy weapons protected by pivoting flaps. Speculum historiae by Vincent de Beauvais, circa 1463.**
*(Paris, Bibl. nat. de France Ms. Fr. 50 f° 353 v°)*

*Opposite, on the right.* **The mythical siege of Carohaise. The powder artillery did not immediately eliminate the traditional arsenal of siege warfare. Catapult type weapons continued to be used until the end of the XVth century. Histoire de Merlin, circa 1330.**
*(Paris, Bibl. nat. de France Ms. Fr. 9123 f° 280 v°)*

*"Dull Griet"* (Mad Meg), placed in a Ghent square, five metres tall and a total weight of 36,000 pounds.
*(Photo Serge Lecompte)*

121

*Above.*
**The terrible siege of Sagonte (Spain)**
**by the Carthagian general, Hannibal, 219**
**B.C. The scene shows, as is the custom with**
**medieval illuminations, dress, decorations**
**and anachronistic weapons. The first hand**
**held fire arms, couleuvrines attached**
**to long sticks, used alongside the more**
**classic bows and crossbows.**
**History of Rome, Tite-Live, 2nd quarter**
**of the XVth century.**
*(Paris, Bibl. nat. de France Ms. Fr. 278 f° 1)*

*Opposite, on the right.*
**The English, laying siege to Calais,**
**are attacked in their retrenchments.**
**The best way to bend a town to one's will**
**was to cut it off from the outside world.**
**Wooden bastilles (forts) were built**
**to counter an eventual breakout by the**
**besieged population.**
**Jean Chartier, Chronicles,**
**3rd quarter of the XVth century.**
*(Paris, Bibl. nat. de France Ms. Fr. 2691 f° 121)*

*Opposite page, centre.*
**The siege of Harcourt.**
**The artillery evolved quickly. The heavy**
**pieces were progressively replaced**
**by smaller weapons, capable of firing, with**
**force, calibrated metal cannonballs. Easier**
**to handle, they were mounted on a mobile**
**chassis, whilst the enormous bombardes**
**remained attached to the ground.**
**Vigiles of Charles VII**
**by Martial d'Auvergne, 1484.**
*(Paris, Bibl. nat. de France*
*Ms. Fr. 5054 f° 161 v°)*

*Opposite page, centre.*
**Philippe Auguste attacks**
**Le Mans or Tours at the end of the XIIth**
**century. The illumination, however,**
**dates from the end of the XIVth century**
**and the warriors are equipped according**
**to what was in use at this time.**
**The crossbow remained the favourite**
**personal weapon during the sieges of all**
**of the Hundred Years War, this was due**
**to its power and formidable accuracy.**
**Grandes Chroniques de France, circa 1380.**
*(Bibl. mun. de Lyon, Ms P.A. 30 f° 235 v°.*
*Photographs Bibliothèque*
*municipale de Lyon, Didier Nicole)*

**The well kept the fortress supplied with water.**
**Castle of Chinon.**

explosive mixture to be fired. Thus heated, the powder exploded and brutally shot out the projectile. The violent recoil was absorbed by the wooden case.

## Lowering costs and technological improvements.

In order to amplify the destructive power of the cannons, scientists firstly increased the size of the weapons. Cannons weighing 6,000, 10,000 and 15,000 pounds became relatively common in the princely arsenals. These weapons were capable, from very early on, to fire cannonballs weighing 200, 300 or even 400 pounds. There were, however, several hefty drawbacks. We have already mentioned their lack of reliability to which should be added the lack of manœuvrability and doubtful precision. The quality of the powder also turned out to be very mediocre. The (very expensive) saltpetre and the sulphur were heavier and denser than the wood charcoal. Consequently they often settled at the bottom of the barrels during transportation. This had a considerable effect on its efficiency.

At the beginning of the XVth century, the process of the powder's granulation was perfected. The three ingredients were now perfectly blended. Transportation no longer posed any real problem and using the powder was less dangerous and its efficiency increased. Weapons also began to be cast in one piece. This meant that they were more solid and safer to use. The manufacture of these cannons in greater numbers allowed for a decrease in production costs. Smaller and more easily used *batons à feux* (the ancestor of the musket) appeared. Weapons of average calibre like *veuglaires* (a type of *bombarde*) and culverins, appeared out of nowhere, considerably adding to the defensive potential of a fortress. Jean Mesqui quite rightly says that the widespread use of the latter lead to arrow slits having holes bored in their centre as has been previously mentioned. There was no longer any hesitation in using these news weapons in battles in the open field. Charles VII, owed a large part of his success at Castillon (1453), the last great battle of the Hundred Years War, to the way in which mobile artillery was used, thought up by the Bureau brothers.

Strategists, however, refused to use these latest technological advances exclusively. They kept their faith in more traditional weaponry such as mangonels and trebuchets, despite their high cost, wear and size. Froissart spoke of a siege engine next to two firearms at the siege of Audenarde in Belgium, *"a wooden machine that was called 'mouton' throwing stones into the town bringing everything down."* He even gives us the size of this 'mouton': a surface area of 6,50 by 13 metres and 6,50 metres in height. The accounts of the Dauphin Charles for 1421, show the sum of 160 pounds, paid to maitre Jean Thibaut for two machines known as *couillards*. Twenty years later, in 1442, Monstrelet

described precisely the attack by the English on Conches-en-Ouche. *"Nientmains elle fut très fort approuchiée et assaillie, tant de canons comme d'aultres groz engiens et habillemens de guerre. Et tellement fut contrainte, que de jour en jour, ceulx de dedens faisoient grand doubte d'estre prins d'assault"*.[2]

These *"groz engiens"* (large siege engines) and *"habillemens"* (instruments), that allowed a full scale bombardment, do not seem to designate firearms, already mentioned under the generic term of cannons. Finally, in the field of personal weapons, the crossbow remained the favourite choice by both the attackers and the besieged. It was only considered obsolete in the first decades of the XVIth century.

## The siege is all about patience

This arsenal was, however, only part of the techniques of siege and attack. It allowed for an easier bombardment of the walls, creating breaches thanks to its firepower. Firing with a curved trajectory, it could bombard building behind the walls, breaking open roofs and demoralizing the besieged population. Ladders, battering rams, cats, siege towers and saps were still popular with strategists. Assaults still had a large appetite for… human flesh. In fact it was very often a lack of food and fear of being massacred that made the besieged population lay down their arms. Monstrelet tells how, for example, the Duke of Bedford made Château-Gaillard surrender in 1429, after six to seven months of siege, *"because they were without food"*.

To sum up, taking a fortress 'chastel' or a 'good town' required as much know how, means and… patience, as before. Vegece's old saying does not beat about the bush and still rings true: *"Hunger will prevail more often than iron!"*.  ❑

2. *"So it was violently attacked and assaulted, with canons as well as other instruments of war. It was so heavily harrassed that, as the days went by, those that were shut inside thought they were being assaulted."*

# Bibliography

Jean Favier and his indispensable book, the *Guerre de Cent Ans* (Fayard, Paris 1993), has been our companion throughout the study of the period in question.

This book of some 650 pages is an excellent summary of the subject's essential points.

A great effort has been made in recent years to reprint ancient texts. *Les Editions des Belles Lettres* and more recently, the *Lettres Gothiques* collection, by Livre de Poche, have greatly worked towards this end. It should be noted that the latter has recently published the shortened version of *Jean Foissart's* delightful *Chronicles* in four books (Paris, 2001 and 2004).

Froissart exhibits the fervour of a falsely naive teenager.

Spicy!

For the complete text and valuable appendix, the reader would do well to refer to *Baron K. de Lettenhove's publication* of twenty five volumes (Brussels, 1867-77).

On the other hand, the second great French historian of the Hundred Years War, for the period of 1400-1444, Enguerrand de Monstrelet, still awaits a publisher. We referred to the old publication of his *Chroniques*, by L. Douet-d'Arcq (Paris, 1857-62).

For the history of the fortifications, the author of this study, Stéphane William Gondoin, published *Les Châteaux Forts,* with Cheminements (Coudray-Macouard, 2005).

We also invite you to consult the *Dictionnaire des châteaux et fortifications du Moyen Age en France*, by Charles-Laurent Salch, published by Publitotal (Strasbourg, 1979) and *Châteaux forts et fortifications en France* by Jean Mesqui, Flammarion (Paris, 1997).

One of the best books currently available on siege techniques is *The Medieval Siege* by Jim Boydell, Boydell Press (Woodbridge, 1992).

In French, there is the interesting *Art de la Guerre au Moyen Age* by Renaud Beffeyte, Ouest-France (Rennes, 2005).

On the internet, you can gain further information at *www.richesheures.net*, for whom Stéphane William Gondoin is the chief editor.The following books have ample bibliographies.

### Common works
— Babelon Jean-Pierre, *Le château en France*. Paris, Editions Berger-Levrault et Caisse Nationale des Monuments Historiques et des Sites, 1986.
— Barde Yves, Histoire de la fortification en France.- Paris: PUF, 1996.
— Baylé Maylis, *L'architecture normande au Moyen Age*. Caen, Editions Charles Corlet et Presses universitaires de Caen, 1997.
— Carraz Damien, *L'architecture médiévale en occident*. Paris, PUF, 1999.
— Contamine Phillip, *La Guerre au Moyen Age*. Paris, PUF, 1994.
— Denizeau Pierre, *Larousse des châteaux*. Paris, Larousse, 2005.
— Gravett Christopher, *Medieval siege warfare*. Oxford, Osprey Publishing, 1990.
— Kaufmann J. E. & Kaufmann H. W. *The Medieval Fortress*. London, Greenhill Books, 2001.
— Mesqui Jean, *Les châteaux forts de la guerre à la paix*. Paris, Gallimard, 1995.
— Mesqui Jean, *Châteaux d'Orient*. Paris: Grand Livre, 2001.
— Viollet le Duc Eugène, *Encyclopédie Médiévale*. Bayeux, Inter Livres, 1978.

### Out of print books, specialist articles, monographs
— Affolter Eric et Voisin Jean-Claude, *L'enceinte circulaire du Chas-tel Messire Girard à Fontenois les Montbozon (Haute-Saône)*. Archéologie Médiévale tome XVII, 1987, pp. 105-126.
— Châtelain André, *Evolution des château forts dans la France au Moyen Age*. Strasbourg, Publitotal, 1988.
— Gardelles Jacques, *Le château féodal dans l'histoire médiévale*. Strasbourg, Publitotal, 1988.
— Lonchambon Catherine, *Tarascon. Entre austérité et élégance*. Histoire Médiévale No 27, mars 2002.
— Mesqui Jean, *La fortification des portes avant la guerre de Cent Ans*. Archéologie Médiévale, tome XI, 1981, pp. 203-229.
— Ribaldone Thierry, *La chevalerie et les chevaliers brigands de la France au Moyen Age*. Strasbourg, Publitotal, 1988.
— Salamagne Alain, *Pour une approche typologique de l'architecture militaire: l'exemple de la famille monumentale des tours-portes de plan curviligne*, Archéologie Médiévale, tome XVIII, 1988, pp. 179-213.
— Salch Charles-Laurent, *Les plus beaux châteaux forts en France*. Strasbourg, Publitotal, 1978.
— Salch Charles-Laurent, *Atlas des villes et villages fortifiés en France* (from eve of the du Vth century to the end of the XVth century). Strasbourg, Publitotal, 1987.
— Salch Charles-Laurent, *Atlas des châteaux forts en France*. Strasbourg, Publitotal, 1988.
— Tealdi Jacques, *La France médiévale: romantisme et renouveau*. Strasbourg, Publitotal, 1988.

# Acknowledgements

Cyrille CASTELLANT (*richesheures. com*), Serge LECOMPTE, Didier FAURE, WILD, Emmanuel NAUD,
William GONDOIN, Carole PARNASO (Musée des Beaux-Arts de Dijon), Fabian FORNI (Mairie de Dijon),
Anne-Bérangère ROTHENBURGE (Bibliothèques d'Amiens Métropole)
Daniel BLANCHARD (Office de Tourisme et de Thermalisme de Bourbon-l'Archambault),
Marie-Jeanne BOISTARD (Bibliothèque des Quatre-Piliers, Bourges),
l'association "Escola Gaston Febus".

# Glossary

**Arrow slits.** Thin vertical apertures in a fortification through which an archer could fire in relative safety.

**Ballista.** Engine resembling a crossbow, used in hurling missiles or large arrows.

**Barbican.** A fortification in front of the gatehouse.

**Bartizan.** A small turret of look out post.

**Berzy-le-Sec: a murder hole above the gate.**

**Bombarde.** Steel tube that fired crossbow bolts, lead balls or red hot steel. Larger calibres could fire stone projectiles.

**Bretèche.** A stone machicolation that was placed over a window or doorway.

**Buttress.** A projection supporting a wall.

**Canonnier.** A round or oval port built into a wall - the natural successor to arrow slits after the introduction of firearms.

**Castrum.** Originally a temporary Roman camp. In the Middle Ages this expression designated a fortified position — often on a height — which, unlike a castle, always included a group of dwellings.

**Cat.** A covered battering ram.

**Chevauchée.** The medieval term for

*French and English archeological and medieval terms published in this book*

a particularly destructive kind of military raid especially prominent during The Hundred Years War (and especially used by Edward III of England).

**Corbel.** A support of either stone or wood used on parapets and machicolations.

**Couillard.** A type of counterweight catapult.

**A bretèche at the castle of Chinon.**

**A bretèche visible on the walls of the castle of Saumur.**

**Crenel.** Opening between merlons.

**Culverin.** A long cannon.

**Curtain.** Walls between towers.

**Donjon.** The French term for a castle keep.

**Enceinte.** The defensive walls around a castle.

**Machicolation.** A projecting gallery, built in stone on top of a defensive wall, that allowed defenders to shoot down at besiegers, or drop things onto them.

**Mangonel.** A type of catapult.

**Motet.** Short sacred choral composition.

**Murder hole.** A defensive opening through which defenders could shoot attackers, or drop things on them.

**Palissade.** A wooden fence usually built to enclose a site, made up of a succession of stakes, more or less closely joined, and driven into the ground.

**Perrier.** A type of catapult that used

**The latrines at Bonaguil.**

man or animal power instead of a counterweight to launch the projectile.

**Portcullis.** A grid like gate.

**Ravelin.** Large defensive work, generally triangular or lozenge shaped, and filled with earth, designed to protect a vulnerable point, such as a door, from direct fire.

**Trebuchet.** A military siege engine used for throwing large stones.

**Trouvère.** A medieval epic poet in Northern France.

**Troubadour.** A French medieval lyric poet.

**Vantail.** A small window that could be opened from the inside to see who was outside.

**Latrines at Chinon.**

# French castles of the Hundred Years War

**Château d'Angers**
2, promenade du Bout-du-Monde
49100 Angers
☎ + 33 (0) 2. 41. 86. 48. 77.
http://www.monum.fr

**Château d'Annecy**
Place du château
74000 Annecy
☎ + 33 (0) 4. 50. 33. 87. 30.
http://www.ville-annecy.fr

**Palais des Papes d'Avignon**
6, rue Pente Rapide
Charles Ansidei
84000 Avignon
☎ +33 (0) 4 90 27 50 00
http://www.palais-des-papes.com

**Château de Berzy-le-Sec**
*At the moment this site can only be viewed from the outside*

**Château de Blandy-les-Tours**
77115 Blandy-les-Tours
☎ + 33 (0) 1.60.69.96.89

**Château de Bourbon-l'Archambault**
Office du tourisme
1, place de l'Hotel-de-Ville
03160 Bourbon-l'Archambault
☎ +33 (0) 4. 70. 67. 09. 79
http://www.ot-bourbon.com

**Château de Caen**
14000 Caen
☎ + 33 (0) 2. 31. 30. 47. 60.
http://www.château. caen. fr

**Abbaye de La Chaise-Dieu**
Office du tourisme
43160 La Chaise-Dieu
☎ + 33 (0) 4. 71. 00. 01. 16.
http://www.abbaye-chaise-dieu.com

**Château de Chambéry**
*Currently houses the offices of the prefecture and the departmental administration.*
Office du tourisme
24 boulevard Colonne
73000 Chambéry
☎ + 33 (0) 4. 79. 33. 42. 47.
http://www.mairie-chambery.fr

**Château de Chinon**
Forteresse royale de Chinon
37500 Chinon
☎ +33 (0) 2. 47. 93. 13. 45.
http://www.forteresse-chinon.fr

**Château de Clisson**
44190 Clisson
☎ + 33 (0) 2.40.54.02.22.
http://www.clisson.com

**Château de Crouy-sur-Ourcq**
*At the moment, this site can only be viewed from the outside*

**Château de Curemonte**
*At the moment, this site can only be viewed from the outside*
http://www.curemonte.org

**Palais des Etats de Bourgogne**
21000 Dijon
☎ + 33 (0) 3. 80. 74. 52. 70.
http://www.dijon.fr

**Château de Falaise**
14700 Falaise
☎ + 33 (0) 2. 31. 90. 17. 26.
http://www.falaise.fr

**Château de La Ferté-Milon**
*The facade of Louis d'Orléans' château can be visited above the town.*

**Château de Foix**
09000 Foix
☎ + 33 (0) 5. 34. 09. 83. 83.
http://www.ot-foix.fr

**Fort la Latte**
28 place des Lices
35000 Rennes
☎ +33 (0) 2. 96. 41. 57. 11.
http://www.castlelalatte.com

**Château de Largöet-en-Elven**
56250 Elven
☎ + 33 (0) 2. 97. 53. 35. 96.
http://forteresselargoet.free.fr

**Château de Laval**
Place de la Trémoille
53000 Laval
☎ + 33 (0) 2. 43. 53. 39. 89.
http://www.mairie-laval.fr

**Château-Musée du Louvre**
75058 Paris Cedex 01
☎ + 33 (0) 1. 40. 20. 55. 55.
Internet: http://www.louvre.fr

**Château de Mauvezin**
20 rue du Château
65130 Mauvezin
☎ + 33 (0) 5. 62. 39. 10. 27.
http://www.chateaudemauvezin.com

**Château de Mehun-sur-Yèvre**
Office du tourisme
Place du 14 juillet
18500 Mehun-sur-Yèvre
☎ + 33 (0) 2. 48. 57. 35. 51.
http://perso.orange.fr/office-tourisme-mehun-sur-yevre

**Tours de Merle**
19220 Saint-Geniez-O-Merle
☎ + 33 (0) 5. 55. 28. 22. 31.
http://www.st-geniez-o-merle.com

**Château de Montaner**
Bourg
64460 Montaner
☎ + 33 (0) 5. 59. 38. 05. 86.
http://www.château-montaner. info

**Château de Montreuil-Bellay**
49260 Montreuil-Bellay
☎ + 33 (0) 2.41.52.33.06.
http://www.château-de-montreuil-bellay. fr

**Château de Montsoreau**
BP 19
49730 Montsoreau
☎ + 33 (0) 2. 41. 67. 12. 60.
www.château-montsoreau. com

**Château de Pierrefonds**
60350 Pierrefonds
☎ + 33 (0) 3. 44. 42. 72. 72.
http://www.monum.fr

**Château de Poitiers**
*The Great Hall has been re-named 'La Salle des Pas Perdus' (The Hall of the Lost Steps) and is part of the law courts.*
Office du tourisme
45 Place Charles De Gaulle
☎ + 33 (0) 5. 49. 41. 21. 24.
http://www.ot-poitiers.fr

**Château de Polignac**
43000 Polignac
☎ + 33 (0) 4. 71. 04. 06. 04
http://www.ot-lepuyenvelay.fr

**Château de Pouzauges**
Mairie
85700 Pouzauges
☎ + 33 (0) 2. 51. 57. 01. 37.
http://www.pouzauges.com

**Château de Rochebaron**
43210 Bas en Basset
☎ + 33 (0) 4. 71. 61. 80. 44.
http://www.rochebaron.org

**Château de Saint-Mesmin**
La Ville
79380 Saint André sur Sèvre
☎ +33 (0) 5. 49. 74. 52. 47.
http://www.ebusinessgeneration.net/château-saintmesmin

**Château de Saint-Sauveur-le-Vicomte**
Office du Tourisme
Le Vieux Château
50390 Saint-Sauveur-le-Vicomte
☎ + 33 (0) 2.33.21.50.44)
http://www.saintsauveurlevicomte.fr.st/

**Château de Saumur**
49400 Saumur
☎ + 33 (0) 2. 41. 40. 24. 40.
http://www.saumur.fr

**Château de Septmonts**
33 rue des Allées
02200 Septmonts
☎ + 33 (0) 3. 23. 74. 95. 35.

**Château de Sully-sur-Loire**
45600 Sully-sur-Loire.
☎ + 33 (0) 2. 38. 36. 36. 86.
Internet: http://www.sully-sur-loire.fr

**Château de Suscinio**
56370 Sarzeau
☎ + 33 (0) 2. 97. 41. 91. 91.
http://www.suscinio.info

**Château de Tancarville**
*The castle can be partially seen from the outside.*

**Château de Tarascon**
13150 Tarascon
☎ + 33 (0) 4. 90. 91. 01. 93.
http://www.monum.fr

**Château de Tiffauges**
BP14
85130 Tiffauges
☎ + 33 (0) 2. 51. 65. 70. 51.
http://château-barbe-bleue.vendee. fr

**Château de Tonquédec**
22140 Tonquédec
☎ + 33 (0) 2. 96. 54. 60. 70.

**Châteaux
de Villeneuve-lès-Avignon**
30400 Villeneuve-lès-Avignon

**Tour Phillip the Fair**
☎ + 33 (0) 4. 32. 70. 08. 57.

**Fort Saint-André**
☎ + 33 (0) 4. 90. 25. 45. 35.
http://www.villeneuvelesavignon.fr

**Château de Vincennes**
Avenue de Paris
94300 Vincennes
☎ + 33 (0) 1 48 08 31 20
http://www.château-vincennes. fr

**Château de Vitré**
35500 Vitré
☎ + 33 (0) 2. 99. 75. 04. 54.
http://www.ot-vitre.fr/

# French castles of the Hundred Years War

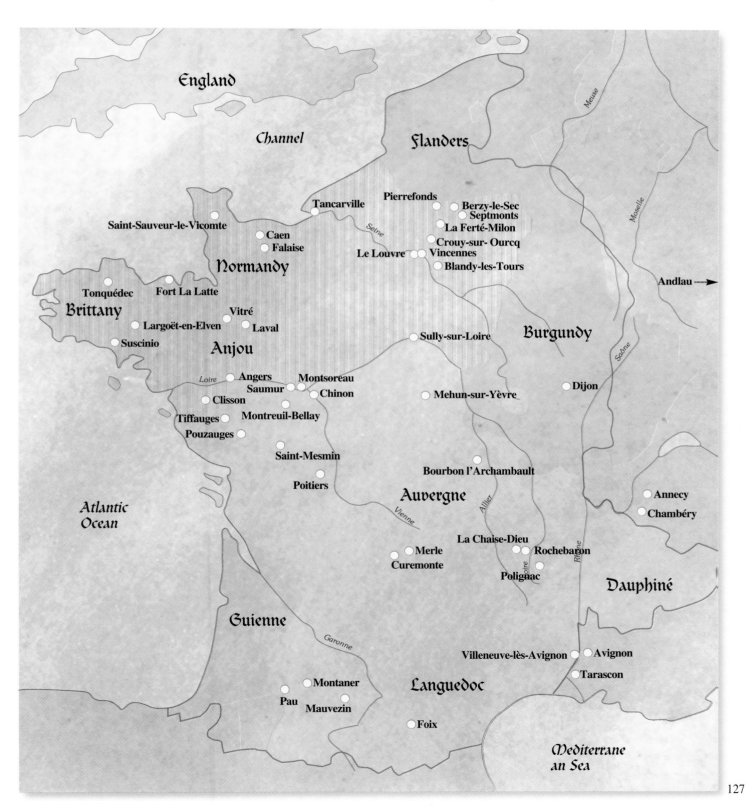

England

Channel

Flanders

Meuse

Moselle

Tancarville

Pierrefonds

Berzy-le-Sec
Septmonts
La Ferté-Milon
Crouy-sur- Ourcq
Vincennes
Blandy-les-Tours

Seine

Le Louvre

Saint-Sauveur-le-Vicomte

Caen
Falaise

Normandy

Andlau →

Tonquédec

Fort La Latte

Brittany

Vitré

Laval

Burgundy

Largoët-en-Elven

Suscinio

Anjou

Sully-sur-Loire

Saône

Loire

Angers
Saumur

Montsoreau
Chinon

Mehun-sur-Yèvre

Dijon

Clisson

Tiffauges

Montreuil-Bellay

Pouzauges

Saint-Mesmin

Bourbon l'Archambault

Poitiers

Auvergne

Atlantic
Ocean

Vienne

Allier

Annecy

Chambéry

La Chaise-Dieu

Rochebaron

Merle

Curemonte

Loire

Polignac

Rhône

Dauphiné

Guienne

Garonne

Villeneuve-lès-Avignon

Avignon

Tarascon

Montaner

Pau

Mauvezin

Languedoc

Foix

Mediterrane
an Sea

Viollet le Duc liked to sign his work by [...]
a sculpture in his image. He can be seen [...]
a *Jacquet* (a Saint-Jacques of Compostelle pi[...]
Castle of Pierre[...]